ROOT

ROOTS in IRAN

Stories of Visionary Women

Written by

YASMINE MAHDAVI

Illustrated by

STEPHANIE BADR | SAMAR CHAHINE | ROSANE CHAWI |
SAHAR HAGHGOO | CHRISTELLE HALAL |
ZAYNAB KADRI | DALIDA RAAD

Illustrations were created by Stephanie Badr (Kimia Alizadeh, Mina Bissell, Melody Ehsani, Katayoun Khosrowyar), Samar Chahine (Anousheh Ansari, Dorsa Derakhshani), Rosane Chawi (Shirin Ebadi, Farnaz Esmaeilzadeh, Maryam Mirzakhani), Sahar Haghgoo (Golshifteh Farahani, Shirin Neshat, Marjane Satrapi), Christelle Halal (Jasmin Moghbeli, Niaz Kasravi, ACT(ivism)), Zaynab Kadri (Anna Eskamani, Yasmine Mahdavi), and Dalida Raad (Iran-Iraq War, Pep Talk, Women in Chess, Veiled, Notable Women, Life on ISS, Nowruz, Space Studies).

Published in the United States by Drummer Media, Inc.
Library of Congress Cataloging-in-Publication data available.

Paperback ISBN: 9780578965000

With love for
My parents, Iraj and Shahla Mahdavi, immigrant trailblazers
who paved the way for Sarvy and me,
and
Ian, Charlotte, and Patrick.

CONTENTS

PROLOGUE

I grew up in Iran until I was twelve. In Tehran, I was surrounded by my extended family—grandparents, uncles, aunts, and cousins. Our privileged life was lost on me until we moved to the U.S.; in Tehran, we had a four-bedroom apartment on a forked road, with a private yard where my dad hoisted a homemade swing for my sister and me. In our garage, to my delight, we often found stray cats.

On the weekends, we escaped Tehran's hustle and bustle for the country, where my parents owned acres of land covered with apple trees. There, we had a modest house, a pool, horses, and chickens. A quiet, gentle Afghan man, with deep wrinkles that aged him beyond his years, took care of the property. My heart ached when I learned that unrest in Afghanistan had forced him to flee his beloved country.

On hot days, my sister and I swam in the pool's ice-cold waters and explored the hilly grounds, finding snakeskins, and green-and-brown turtles hiding in their shells. Until the 1979 Islamic Revolution, I attended Iranzamin, a private American school in Tehran, where my mom was a teacher.

That revolution—which overthrew the ham-fisted monarchy and instated an authoritarian theocracy—and the subsequent war with Iraq changed my life, as it did the lives of tens of millions of others, including many of the heroines in this book. I was young and only have a hazy recollection of the revolution. Adults whispered about a "coup d'état" when vague murmurs of another ousted government official were heard.

My memories of the war are more vivid. The windows of our apartment were taped and covered by newspapers to protect us from the flying shrapnel and broken glass that resulted from the bomb raids. In Tehran, students doing homework by candlelight and parents standing in line for food were common. Ear-piercing sirens at night warned us to take shelter from the bombs. I still remember our apartment trembling after a bomb dropped nearby, and, to this day, the sounds of Fourth of July fireworks remind me of the sound of explosions.

During this time, my parents attempted to maintain normalcy. When my eight-year-old sister insisted she wanted to buy bread from a local bread-maker, my dad—fearing bomb raids—escorted her from five feet behind. When Tehran was the least safe, we took days-long refuge at our orchard.

In the early days of the revolution, the hijab (a veil covering a woman's head) became compulsory. The change came swiftly, and refusing to wear one was punishable by law. As a child, I thought this rule didn't make sense. I questioned why the Christian and Muslim God, whom I had been taught were one and the same, had different rules about who had to cover their hair. There seemed to be a human hand, perhaps a man's, in what God wanted women to do.

My pious nanny, whose henna-colored hair peeked out from under her hijab, simply said, "Child, God is the light inside you." Her response made me think that the path to living a moral life came from within and could not be dictated by others in the name of any institution, including religion.

My parents finally left Iran for the U.S., where they had lived as students decades earlier. In Iran, there were few professional opportunities for them and minimal educational prospects for my sister and me. I imagine life had been extremely stressful for them, not least because, soon after our arrival in the U.S., my mom was diagnosed with cancer.

Against this backdrop, when I was the teen-ripening age of twelve, we moved to Southern California. It was spring of 1986, and

California was utterly foreign to me. Even though I spoke fluent English, I stood out in a sea of blonde classmates. I came from a land of rationed food; my classmates had glossy grocery stores with enough food to feed hundreds for days. I had watched grainy black-and-white Indian movies with dreadful themes; they had light and airy sitcoms. On my best days, I wore clothes bought from Sears; they flaunted pricey Guess jeans and pink Reebok high-tops. I was keenly aware of being different.

I belonged to worlds that were often at odds with one another. In this new country, I had to negotiate and renegotiate what it meant to be myself. In the 1980s, there were no public figures in the U.S. who looked like me, no books about children like me, and no one who understood my experiences. Most of my classmates had limited knowledge about my country, and what they did know was unflattering. Some remembered the Iran hostage crisis, when American diplomats were held hostage in Iran for four hundred and forty-four days at the onset of the revolution. Others had seen news coverage of the Iran-Contra hearings with Oliver North.

I was determined to reconcile how I would relate to the world and, in turn, how it would relate to me. But navigating my new homeland was tricky. The mixed emotions that Americans had about Iran encouraged me to strip away parts of my roots and silence others. In a Calculus class, when a blonde, blue-eyed classmate—bitter about not having received a higher test score—mockingly referred to the only other Iranian boy in our class as "those people who are good at math," I stayed quiet about my heritage.

I lived in California until 1999, after which I moved to New York. After graduate school, I began a career, got married, and had two children.

Decades after my arrival to the U.S., as I raise my children, Iran and its people remain shrouded in mystery. I still struggle to find public figures who look like me and have had experiences similar to mine. The lingering misconceptions fan the flames of fear and suspicion. They stain opinions in playgrounds, workplaces, classrooms, and, most dangerously, the voting booths. And the scarcity of notable immigrant Iranian women doesn't disabuse these notions.

Nobel Laureate Toni Morrison once said, "If there is a book that you want to read, but it hasn't been written yet, you must be the one to write it." I wrote this book for my thirteen-year-old self, when I was coming of age in my adopted country while cherishing memories of my homeland, and for my children. I wish I knew back then all of the things I know now.

My wish is that by reading these stories of phenomenal women with roots in Iran, you revel, as I do, in the magnificently complex world we all live in and the humanity we share. I hope peeking into their lives offers you a window into new worlds and a mirror to reflect your own experiences.

LIFE STORIES

انوشه انصاری

ANOUSHEH: IN BRIEF

ANOUSHEH ANSARI lived in Iran until she was sixteen. In her teens, she witnessed protesters demanding the country's monarch end his decades-long reign, and a subsequent war that led to food rations and bomb attacks. Coming of age in revolutionary Iran and living with the destruction of war didn't make her transition to the U.S. easier, but Anousheh persisted. She studied difficult subjects at school, then founded a technology company and sold it for hundreds of millions of dollars. While building her second company, she traveled to the International Space Station (ISS). Anousheh is an intrepid entrepreneur, the first woman to undertake private space travel, and the first person of Iranian ancestry to go into space!

ANOUSHEH ANSARI
b. 1966

*How does a dream of going to space become a reality
for a little girl from Iran?*

It was summer in Tehran, the capital of Iran, and young Anousheh was allowed to sleep on the balcony of her grandparents' house. Fragrant jasmine, growing in pots, perfumed the air as a cool breeze brushed against her cheek. Anousheh lay on her foldout cot, draped with a mosquito net, beside her grandparents, Maman and Buhbuh. She loved spending time at her grandparents' house, but her heart was heavy. Her parents' divorce had shattered her world. Their disagreements led to shouting matches and her mother weeping.

In the darkness, Anousheh felt swathed in the unknown. She stared into the sky, waiting for the night to get darker, and her attention meandered. She pondered how the universe had started and how it would end. Soon, the stars began to wink and twinkle. Anousheh transported herself to deep space and imagined being the boy from her favorite book, *The Little Prince*, the tale of a prince stranded on a distant planet.

She often fantasized about traveling to and from the beautiful stars. She liked to think that they belonged to everyone. Would she one day visit to learn all that she could about them?

Anousheh was born in Mashhad, a city some nine hundred kilometers east of Tehran. Mashhad is considered a holy city because

4

it houses the vast tomb of Imam Reza, who was a descendent of the prophet Muhammad. For Anousheh, the shrine's sparkling golden domes and floodlit minarets evoked the galaxies.

Millions of pilgrims from around the world flocked to the shrine every year. But the city was also home to remarkable thinkers: Sharaf al-Din al-Tusi, a mathematician and astronomer from the Middle Ages, and Ferdowsi, who wrote the world's longest epic poem, *Shahnameh* (The Book of Kings). Was Anousheh fascinated by the night sky because she'd been born in a city of art and science? It certainly wasn't because her parents were interested in astronomy!

Still, Anousheh had been influenced by her family. Her grandparents had a prayer ceremony called the *Sofreh* that helped feed the poor. On those days, the kitchen was filled with pots of rice and stews, and the aromatic smell made Anousheh's mouth water. When she asked her mother why her grandparents were feeding all those people, her mother responded, "People who are blessed with abundance have a duty to help those who are less fortunate."

This idea resonated deeply with Anousheh and went on to light her life's philosophical journey. "Everything I have, I worked very hard to attain," she says, "but I still recognize the need to give back in every way I can."

In her grandparents' kitchen, Anousheh spun around, trying hard to hold in her energy. She tugged at her mother's *chador*, a long cloak that covered her from head to toe, then grabbed a corner and pulled it over herself as if she were an explorer in a cave. Her mother scolded her and told her to start "behaving like a lady."

Anousheh had been reprimanded before for not acting a certain way. Running around and climbing trees were also unladylike activities, and all that was dull—like playing with dolls and kitchen sets—were things a *lady* undertook. She wondered what life would have been like had she been a boy.

When the day was over, Anousheh's exhausted mom continued to answer her questions. Buhbuh, her grandfather, was amused by her inquisitive ways and made up a riddle for her. When she solved it quickly, his face lit up. "You are a smart girl, Anousheh," he said.

Buhbuh was a veterinarian, but he hadn't always been one. Before Reza Shah, the King of Iran, had come to power, Buhbuh's family had been rich. But Buhbuh's father had insulted the Shah, and their family had lost their fortune. Anousheh couldn't imagine what it would be like to be rich. Money was scarce in her family.

———

When Anousheh was four years old, her family moved to Tehran, because her dad thought it might be easier to find a job there. Since Reza Shah had come to power, Iran had become a more prosperous place to live—for some. Modern buildings were being erected and business was thriving.

But when things didn't work out as her dad had planned, he declared the U.S. "the land of opportunity." Anousheh's family sold all their unnecessary belongings to fund her dad's business, selling Iranian handicrafts and rugs. He then moved to the U.S. alone.

His occasional letters didn't feel right. When he moved back to Iran, he asked Anousheh's mom for a divorce. Now, Anousheh had to split her time between her mother's and father's houses and dreaded staying in two places and sorting out new routines.

As the years passed, the state of affairs in Iran became tense. By the time Anousheh was eleven, she was used to hearing rumors of a possible revolution. Open criticisms of the Shah were met with ruthless violence. In 1977, President Carter, on his New Year's Eve visit to Iran, toasted the Shah, saying: "Iran, because of the great leadership of the Shah, is an island of stability in one of the more troubled areas of the world." But weeks later, demonstrations by the Shah's opponents—student activists, communists, democrats, and Islamists—jolted Iran.

Zealous crowds took to the streets, chanting for a change in government and an overthrow of the monarchy. Jittery about the uncertainties, many had started moving assets and money out of the country. Soon after the protests, the 1979 Revolution erupted.

Anousheh wasn't sure what to think about the revolution. A year before, when she'd seen the demonstrators in the street, she had wanted to join in. They wanted a more equitable society! Anousheh felt overjoyed at the thought that ordinary people had the power to make a change in her country. She had seen how poverty had affected some. It was time for a change!

But now, the commotion quickly transitioned from peaceful protests to violence. Anousheh and her mother and sister even had to evacuate their second-floor apartment because vandals set fire to the bank on the ground floor. Those days were scary. In Anousheh's formerly quiet neighborhood, she now heard gunfire and news of people who'd been killed.

She wished with all her heart that things would improve in her country. But things did not get better in Iran. The toppled Iranian monarchy was replaced with a theocracy. And just a year after the revolution, a war with Iraq began.

Anousheh now knew what it was like to sit through air strikes and bomb attacks. There were shortages of food and fuel, and people stood in long queues to buy rice and meat. The electricity went out nearly every night, to obscure the city from enemy bombers. In the dark, Anousheh used a kerosene lantern to do her homework. It was a terrible time with many unknowns, one of which was: Will we survive the night?

As the end of high school neared, Anousheh's prospects of studying astrophysics in college dwindled. After the revolution, during the 1980s, higher education was discouraged for girls. So, when Anousheh's father announced they were moving to the U.S., she felt both relief and sorrow. Leaving the chaos of war was liberating, but how would it feel to part from her loved ones?

◆—◆—◆

Anousheh's move would be far from simple. Since the revolution, diplomatic relations with the U.S. had been practically non-existent. The U.S. no longer had an embassy in Iran. So, Anousheh, her sister, and their father traveled to Germany, a common stopover for many Iranians who needed to line up their immigration paperwork before heading to final destinations like the U.S.

Germany did not feel like a welcoming place to Anousheh. People stared at her and her family with unfriendly glares. Once, Anousheh had been sitting with her sister on a bus when a commotion erupted. A group of German teenagers was pestering a young Turkish mother and her child. One of them picked up the child's stroller, with the toddler still inside, and pushed the mother and stroller off the bus. Anousheh sat up, straight and tense. Surely the driver would intervene or speak sharply to the teenagers! But he didn't say a word. When the bus started moving again, the teenagers laughed and looked around for someone else to harass. Anousheh and her sister huddled deep in their seats and tried to avoid eye contact with them.

As the months in Germany dragged on, Anousheh's misery increased. And when news about their visas finally arrived, it wasn't what they'd been hoping for. Anousheh and her sister had received visas, but their dad had not. So, he returned to Iran while Anousheh's mother joined the girls in Germany to help them continue their applications to come to the U.S.

Finally, after five months in Germany, Anousheh, her mother, and her sister traveled to Washington, D.C., where they were greeted by Anousheh's aunt and uncle.

The U.S. was dramatically different from Iran and Germany! Still, Anousheh remained nervous. For starters, she spoke Farsi (the official language of Iran) and French, but no English. That would have to change if she ever wanted to make a life in her new country, so she enrolled in English as a Second Language classes.

In high school in the U.S., Anousheh heard herself speaking in an uncharacteristically low voice and hunching her shoulders. She still remembered the way people had looked at her in Germany, and she didn't want to call attention to herself. It was her uncle who finally encouraged her to be more confident. He told her that if she worked hard, she would be amazed by how many people would step up to help her, and there would be no limit to what she could achieve.

Slowly, Anousheh allowed herself to believe that things could be better in the U.S. She was a diligent student and excelled in her science and math classes, but she still didn't like her American high school. The kids mocked her accent, and the boys unsettled her. In Iran, after the revolution, boys and girls had attended separate schools. In America, boys and girls shared classrooms, and the boys were often intimidating and made lewd comments about women. With boys around, it seemed the girls were too distracted to focus on their studies. Instead, they obsessed about what they looked like.

Anousheh was lonely. She longed to have a close friend in high school, but to her dismay, she and her classmates seemed to have little in common.

———

Luckily, Anousheh came into her own once she went to college at George Mason University. With her aptitude and stamina for working hard, she studied tough subjects, earning degrees in electrical engineering and computer science. Anousheh felt proud. Back in Iran, her mother had advised her, "Be the master of your life. You should never have to hold out your hand to your husband. Always be prepared to take care of yourself."

Now, Anousheh had graduated from university with both a noteworthy education and the means to reach financial independence. She'd found a good job and gotten married to Hamid. They were doing well — until their jobs relocated and they both had to find new ways of earning a living.

Eventually, Anousheh and her husband found other jobs. All the while, he dreamed of becoming a millionaire before the age of thirty. He was full of ideas for supplementing their income. One was to buy used cars, fix them up, and sell them for a profit. On the weekends, he and Anousheh scoured car auctions and bought the leftovers that large car dealerships didn't want. When they weren't buying cars, they were scrubbing and polishing them for resale. With callous, cracked hands, they would end the weekends only to return to their day jobs on Monday morning.

By this time, Hamid's brother, Amir, had moved to Texas. Missing him, and dissatisfied with their jobs, Hamid and Anousheh decided to set off for Texas too.

There, frustrated again by their tenuous financial situation, Anousheh, Hamid, and Amir met in Hamid's office to brainstorm what to do next. Anousheh said, "We're financing somebody else's company with our own money. We should start our own company!" Amir, standing poised at the whiteboard with a red marker in hand, wrote, "Start our own company."

ABCs of ENTREPRENEURSHIP

Every business you see around you, from the small local restaurant and tech start-up, to large companies like Amazon and Target, began with an entrepreneur. Each entrepreneur saw a need, developed an idea, and organized and operated a business around it. They had a vision. They were willing to take chances, and they were persistent.

Millions of people have new ideas for a business. Entrepreneurs are unique in that they execute their ideas! They are risk-takers.

What does that mean? For one thing, they may lose all of the money they used to start their business — plus anything they may have borrowed! They will make mistakes along the way, but they don't dwell on them. They see their obstacles as a way forward, and they are not afraid to "look stupid."

In fact, persistence may be one of the most important qualities of an entrepreneur. Sometimes, this determination is fueled by their passion, and sometimes, it's simply fueled by necessity. Entrepreneurs often feel that they have no other choice but to succeed.

In the end, entrepreneurs are very proud of the businesses they build. Faced with trials and tribulations, they develop a deeper understanding of who they are.

They formed their new company, called telecom technologies, inc., or "tti" (all in lowercase letters). Hamid was in charge of attracting customers and generating revenue, Amir came up with new products, and Anousheh "kept it all together" as the CEO. She committed herself to mastering the new skills required for her role. She read books, took business and finance classes, and learned how to apply for a small business loan.

After the company had their first breakthrough product, Anousheh became a media sensation. A glamorous photo of her was featured on the cover of *Working Woman*, highlighting her as the winner of the 2000 National Entrepreneurial Excellence Award.

Alas, as she was leading a thriving company, Buhbuh, who was now living in Los Angeles, became ill and Anousheh's uncle was ailing. Anousheh flew to be at their bedside as often as possible. The strain took its toll on both her and Hamid, so eventually Anousheh decided to sell tti.

When Anousheh finally sold her company for a reported hundreds of millions of dollars, she had surpassed her wildest dreams. In 2001, she was listed as one of *Forbes Magazine*'s richest entrepreneurs under the age of forty. But there was still a part of Anousheh that felt unfulfilled — the part of her that had lain on her grandparents' balcony and stared up at the stars. That yearning to go to space still pulsed in her veins.

In early 2000, Anousheh watched Dennis Tito, the first space tourist, being interviewed on TV, and she felt a thrill of excitement. Although she wasn't trained as an astronaut, she realized she could now become a space tourist. The price tag for such an adventure was steep, rumored to be in the millions, but Anousheh finally had the kind of money she needed to pay for it. When asked why she would pay such a price to go into space, Anousheh responded, "How do you put a price on a dream?"

It wasn't until Anousheh met Eric Anderson, the chairman of the company that sent Dennis Tito into space, that her fantasies became a real possibility. Eric told her that his company had made a deal with the Russians to send two private citizens on flights to the ISS. He then invited Anousheh to train in Star City, Russia, for six months. But he told her she would only be training as a backup for

Daisuke "Dice-K" Enomoto, a Japanese businessman. There was no guarantee she would go into space herself. She would just complete the training, and that was all.

There was no hesitation; Anousheh said yes.

Going to space was a dangerous proposition, no matter how diligently one prepared for it. In 2003, the space shuttle *Columbia* had disintegrated upon reentering Earth's atmosphere, and all seven of its crew members had died. Nevertheless, Anousheh knew those crew members had believed in the importance of their endeavor for the future of the world. Kalpana Chawla, one of the astronauts on the *Columbia*, once said, "The path from dreams to success does exist. May [we] have the vision to find it, the courage to get onto it, and the perseverance to follow it." Anousheh drew courage from those words as she packed for her adventure in Star City.

In February 2006, Anousheh traveled to Russia and moved into a small, no-frills apartment. In Russia, she underwent a series of varied and intrusive medical exams. There was an electrocardiogram and an electroencephalograph. At one point, three physicians with three stethoscopes were examining her, and a doctor pulled at her nose so hard that she thought it would tear off. To cope, Anousheh pretended she was in space.

The training regimen was equally grueling. Anousheh participated in many simulations. There was the rotation chair, which reminded her of a medieval torture device, and the "tilt table," an aluminum slab with straps that held down a person's arms and legs. Mimicking the effects of microgravity, either by spinning or causing the fluids to shift in the body, was necessary, but still unpleasant.

Still, Anousheh was glad she was being treated like a real astronaut-in-training. She had heard a story about the first woman cosmonaut to work on the old *Salyut* space station. That woman had been handed an apron and asked to work in the kitchen. Anousheh was glad she was being held to the same standards as the male astronauts. She lifted weights and swam. She also studied Russian, as well as the history and the technical parts of the space station.

Anousheh was enjoying herself, but despite all her hard work, she knew she was still only on standby. As the last few weeks of the training approached, Anousheh prepared to go home. She would be disappointed to not go into space, but still, these past six months had been incredible. She'd learned more about space than she'd ever known before, and she'd formed close friendships with the Russian and American cosmonauts.

One day, three weeks before the scheduled flight date, she received a phone call from Eric. Dice-K had been medically disqualified, and Eric asked her if she wanted to take his spot.

"Are you kidding me? *Of course,* I want to go!"

Anousheh was over the moon! She was finally traveling to her stars.

As an homage to her roots in Iran, she wanted to put a patch of the Iranian flag on her uniform next to the flag of the U.S., her adopted country. She was surprised when her idea was promptly vetoed. The chief of the Russian training program told her that she "couldn't make a political statement" and had to remove the flag.

Saddened by this unexpected controversy, Anousheh tried to stay focused on the space launch.

In September of 2006, Anousheh's dream finally came true. She lifted off on the *Soyuz* TMA-9 mission from Baikonur, Kazakhstan, to travel to the ISS. The journey was just as terrifying and exhilarating as she had expected.

Once she arrived on the space station, which orbited Earth every ninety minutes, Anousheh could see the brilliant view of Earth from space. She wished everyone could see it. From this view, there were no boundaries and no walls on her home planet.

During her weeklong stay on the ISS, Anousheh became deeply absorbed in her work—conducting experiments on the mechanisms behind anemia, muscle influence on lower back pain, consequences of space radiation on the ISS crew, and microbial species living on the ISS.

Anousheh was also learning what it was like to become famous. In Iran, media outlets picked up on her story and were documenting it on the official government Space Agency website. The Iranian astronomer Pouria Nazemi was encouraging his fellow citizens to gather at night and watch the ISS as it passed over Iran's cities. This was exhilarating for Anousheh, even when she was disparaged for pursuing a so-called frivolous adventure or setting a bad example for young Iranian women.

When Anousheh returned to Earth, she brought with her a vision of empathy and unity. No matter which country we come from, she believes, we can work together for a brighter future for our beloved planet. As Anousheh continues with her work and travels around the world, she reminds us to live the message written on her mission patch to the ISS: *Imagine. Be the Change. Inspire.*

Material from this chapter was heavily sourced from Anousheh Ansari's memoir, *My Dream of Stars.*

THE WAR BETWEEN IRAN AND IRAQ
1980–1988

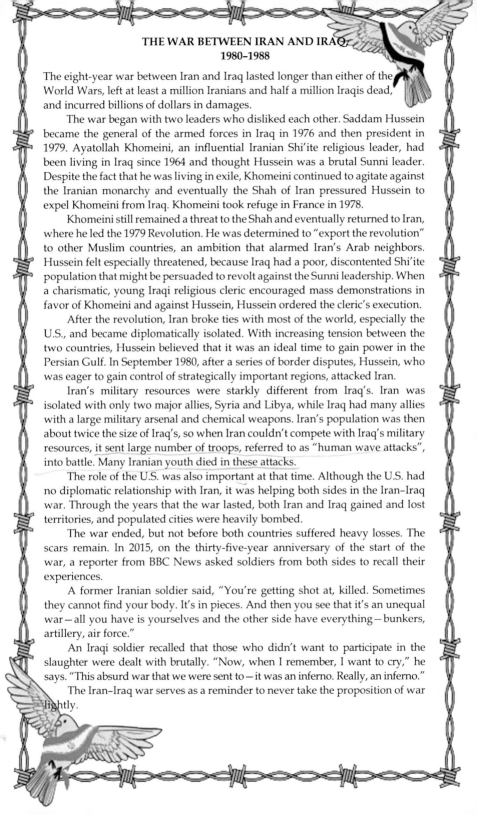

The eight-year war between Iran and Iraq lasted longer than either of the World Wars, left at least a million Iranians and half a million Iraqis dead, and incurred billions of dollars in damages.

The war began with two leaders who disliked each other. Saddam Hussein became the general of the armed forces in Iraq in 1976 and then president in 1979. Ayatollah Khomeini, an influential Iranian Shi'ite religious leader, had been living in Iraq since 1964 and thought Hussein was a brutal Sunni leader. Despite the fact that he was living in exile, Khomeini continued to agitate against the Iranian monarchy and eventually the Shah of Iran pressured Hussein to expel Khomeini from Iraq. Khomeini took refuge in France in 1978.

Khomeini still remained a threat to the Shah and eventually returned to Iran, where he led the 1979 Revolution. He was determined to "export the revolution" to other Muslim countries, an ambition that alarmed Iran's Arab neighbors. Hussein felt especially threatened, because Iraq had a poor, discontented Shi'ite population that might be persuaded to revolt against the Sunni leadership. When a charismatic, young Iraqi religious cleric encouraged mass demonstrations in favor of Khomeini and against Hussein, Hussein ordered the cleric's execution.

After the revolution, Iran broke ties with most of the world, especially the U.S., and became diplomatically isolated. With increasing tension between the two countries, Hussein believed that it was an ideal time to gain power in the Persian Gulf. In September 1980, after a series of border disputes, Hussein, who was eager to gain control of strategically important regions, attacked Iran.

Iran's military resources were starkly different from Iraq's. Iran was isolated with only two major allies, Syria and Libya, while Iraq had many allies with a large military arsenal and chemical weapons. Iran's population was then about twice the size of Iraq's, so when Iran couldn't compete with Iraq's military resources, it sent large number of troops, referred to as "human wave attacks", into battle. Many Iranian youth died in these attacks.

The role of the U.S. was also important at that time. Although the U.S. had no diplomatic relationship with Iran, it was helping both sides in the Iran–Iraq war. Through the years that the war lasted, both Iran and Iraq gained and lost territories, and populated cities were heavily bombed.

The war ended, but not before both countries suffered heavy losses. The scars remain. In 2015, on the thirty-five-year anniversary of the start of the war, a reporter from BBC News asked soldiers from both sides to recall their experiences.

A former Iranian soldier said, "You're getting shot at, killed. Sometimes they cannot find your body. It's in pieces. And then you see that it's an unequal war—all you have is yourselves and the other side have everything—bunkers, artillery, air force."

An Iraqi soldier recalled that those who didn't want to participate in the slaughter were dealt with brutally. "Now, when I remember, I want to cry," he says. "This absurd war that we were sent to—it was an inferno. Really, an inferno."

The Iran–Iraq war serves as a reminder to never take the proposition of war lightly.

مینا
بیسل

MINA: IN BRIEF

MINA BISSELL moved to the U.S. when she was eighteen to attend college on a merit scholarship. She found her element in chemistry, received an award for her work, and moved on to complete her doctorate and post-doctorate work in bacterial genetics, all while raising two children. This rebel broke scientific barriers and turned the world of cancer research on its head with her novel ideas.

MINA BISSELL

b. 1940

How does a girl born in Iran during the second World War become a world-renowned research scientist in California?

Eight-year-old Mina loved climbing trees. One day, while jumping on a high bar set by her fifteen-year-old cousin between two columns over a hard surface, Mina fell. It was devastating. After that, the vivacious, Joan-of-Arc-loving Mina was confined to her bed for months to heal from her injuries.

She eventually recovered, but the fall caused her to lose the hearing in her left ear, as well as most of her photographic memory. She was reminded of this loss while studying Arabic and English in high school, when she had difficulty remembering names and places.

Not all was lost, though. Before the fall, the adults in her life had been amused by Mina's memory and used to test her for fun. The uncomfortable attention she received from them caused her to shy away from her peers. In a way, the calamities of that carefree day brought her out of her shell. Where previously all she'd wanted to do was hide behind her books, she now became more social and even attended ballet classes. Her memories from those ballet classes at age ten are some of her favorites, even though she never mastered the splits!

When Mina reflected on that time in her life, years later, she said, "Despite the injury, I felt better integrated after recovery! Persians have a saying that I often still repeat: 'Enemy can bring good, if goodness is willing!'"

Mina's childhood took place at a fragile time in Iran's history. She was born in Tehran in 1940, when Iran was still under the reign of a monarch, Reza Pahlavi — also known as Reza Shah. When Mina was around a year old, Reza Shah was abruptly removed from the throne and his twenty-two-year-old son, Mohammad Reza, was crowned. World War II was also raging, and it was taking a heavy toll on Iran. The British and the Soviets had gained control of Iranian roads and railways. Food was scarce, in part as a result of bad harvests. And the country's resources were strained as large numbers of European refugees fleeing their homelands entered Iran.

WHY DID A KING GIVE UP HIS THRONE?

Reza Shah came to power in Iran in 1925, after toppling the previous monarch and declaring himself "Shah" (king). Before and after assuming the throne, he introduced many radical changes to Iranian society. Some of his most important reforms were educational reforms (including the establishment of a modern university), elevating the rights and status of women, and building new roads and railroads. Reza Shah also wanted fair trade agreements with the two foreign powers that most influenced his country: Britain and the Soviet Union.

Although Reza Shah strived to maintain positive relations with both Britain and the Soviet Union, it grew increasingly difficult to do so once World War II began. Britain and the Soviet Union, who were now allies in the war against Germany, began to make demands on Iran. They wanted Iran to provide logistical support for the war and to expel all Germans who had been living and working in Iran.

Because Reza Shah did not cooperate with their demands, Britain and the Soviet Union invaded Iran in 1941. This attack was called the Anglo-Soviet Invasion. The Soviets took hold of the northern part of Iran while the British controlled the south. Using this chaotic time to their advantage, the British sought to weaken Reza Shah's power. They asked Reza Shah, "Would His Highness kindly abdicate in favor of his son, the heir to the throne? We have a high opinion of him and will ensure his position. But His Highness should not think there is any other solution."

Reza Shah didn't really have any other choice but to abdicate. The British were, politely, demanding his resignation. His young son, Mohammad Reza, was crowned the new Shah of Iran. The British exiled Reza Shah to South Africa, where he died in 1944.

Despite the country's destruction, Mina grew up happily in her large, middle-class family. Her father was the oldest of ten children, and he and his siblings were passionate about education, literature, and politics. Even though education for women in Iran expanded in the earlier part of the twentieth century, in 1922, the number of female students in school was a small fraction of male students — 7,200 compared to 35,000. Despite this, all of Mina's aunts were college educated. One even had a PhD in French literature from the Sorbonne, a prestigious university in Paris!

From a very young age, Mina had been encouraged to attain intellectual enlightenment and financial autonomy. Her mother was adamant about this. Mina knew that not having finished college sometimes made her mother feel inadequate. Her mother didn't like relying on Mina's father for everything.

Mina excelled in school, and science was especially interesting to her. In her last year of high school, she received the top academic scores, and Mohammad Reza Shah granted her an award to study abroad.

Receiving the scholarship was splendid! It wasn't common for a student from Iran to study at a world-renowned university. Mina wanted to come to the U.S., but her father thought it was "too young a country to educate women." But Mina's paternal grandfather championed Mina's idea. "She has earned it, she is good, and she deserves to go wherever she wants!" he said. And so, Mina's father eventually acquiesced to her request.

Mina's grandfather was truly special. She loved him deeply, for he was an enlightened man. He was an ayatollah, a high-ranking religious cleric, who was an expert in Islamic studies. His influence helped fulfill Mina's dreams of attending college in the U.S.

———

Barely eighteen years old, and knowing only an uncle who lived in New York, Mina moved to the U.S. to attend Bryn Mawr, a women's liberal arts college in Pennsylvania. In the early years, Mina often felt homesick. It was lonely being in a new country all by herself. Still, she remained laser-focused on her studies. Eventually, she transferred to Radcliffe College, Harvard's sister school, to be closer to her fiancé, who was enrolled at Harvard. She found her element in chemistry.

Mina intended to return to Iran once she earned her degree in 1963. But her Iranian husband, whom she married soon after graduating, was still working on his PhD, so she decided to stay in the U.S. and enter the bacterial genetics doctorate program at Harvard Medical School.

Her chosen area of study and career path would be a tough road. She was one of only three women in Harvard's graduate program that year. During that time, only one woman served on the Harvard faculty. Not too long before that, in 1956, Ruth Bader Ginsberg had been one of nine women, in a class of five hundred, enrolled at Harvard Law School. You may even recall that Ruth and her female classmates were famously asked to justify taking class seats away from men!

Still, Mina was determined to succeed, and so she remained in the bacterial genetics program.

Soon after starting graduate school, Mina got pregnant. Her advisor, Luigi Gorini, who chose to work with Mina after she had answered a challenging physics question in a high-resolution microscopy class, was not pleased. "What would your mother say?" he asked, implying that her parents would expect her to quit graduate school because of the pregnancy. "My mother and father called from Iran to make sure I would not be quitting," she replied.

Mina felt encouraged by her research. While everyone else in the lab was focused on a trending topic — antibiotics resistance — she began to create her own niche and used her background in chemistry to propel her work.

One evening, when her daughter was still a baby, Mina became excited as she pored over her data. This was it! She'd just gained an important insight about proteins. But when she showed her results to Luigi, he wasn't impressed. He snapped at her, saying, "What do you think this protein is? Spaghetti? Perhaps you should go back to ballet dancing, because you will not succeed as a scientist."

She felt dejected. Was he implying that her idea was as inconsequential as simply cooking pasta in hot water?

Mina felt that Luigi had perhaps lost faith in her abilities after she'd had a child, so she sought the guidance of another professor on how to handle Luigi's rejection of her work.

The professor listened patiently. "You may or may not be right about his lack of faith in you, but I think Luigi's reaction is because your hypothesis is too 'radical.' He is not convinced by your data and your explanation. You are challenging conventional wisdom and going out on a limb, so the burden of proof is on you," he said matter-of-factly. "Instead of feeling annoyed, you should troubleshoot and do further experiments to prove your point beyond a reasonable doubt."

Mina mulled this over. When she returned to the lab, she was determined to show Luigi more proof to back up her idea.

By way of background, proteins — not so much the nutrients in the foods we eat as much as the microscopic, workhorse molecules inside cells — are made up of a string of a variety of amino acids. This string of amino acids folds into a three-dimensional shape, which allows a protein to become functional. Since the process of folding is marvelously complicated, it can fail, and this failure can lead to diseases.

Mina correctly hypothesized that, given calcium's structural and chemical properties, its presence could help proteins fold correctly. Calcium is an element that plays many roles inside and outside of a cell, including as a signal to initiate processes within a cell. Mina's advisor had a perfectly reasonable hypothesis that calcium served as a signal for the protein to be secreted. However, after looking at her data, Mina had an alternate, completely new hypothesis: that calcium stabilized the protein as it was folding. About a year later, she showed Luigi the proof for her theory, and he became a firm believer in her discovery.

Mina's idea was received harshly at first. But the onus of having bulletproof testing remained hers. This important realization continued to pave the way for her future discoveries.

———•———

In 1970, Mina and her family moved to California. She had read about Harry Rubin, a biology professor at the University of California, Berkeley, and become fascinated by his work. Intrigued, she began an American Cancer Society Fellowship in his lab. She then went on to work as a post-doctoral fellow in a chemistry lab.

When she showed up to her first day of work, Mina was eager to embark on all the research she had been thinking about. But when her supervisor saw that she was seven months pregnant, this time with her son, he told her to go back home. Pregnant women were apparently not welcome in the lab.

Mina was frustrated. This wasn't the first time she'd been dismissed as a scientist. She remembered how, early in her career, a manager had intentionally stifled her ambitions by refusing to sign her grant applications. She was annoyed to find that now, as qualified as she was, people were still making judgments about her as a scientist.

Nevertheless, she decided to persevere at her job, with Calvin Melvin, a Nobel Laureate, as her mentor.

One day, she disagreed with Melvin about a finding, and he blew up at her. Instead of becoming distressed, Mina looked him right in the eye and said, "I disagree with you sometimes, but not because I'm being difficult. You know so much more than I do, but I just know a bit more about biology — so why be so angry all the time?"

Melvin was taken aback. After that encounter, Mina noticed that

23

he became much friendlier toward her. Melvin ended up becoming her close colleague and a champion of her work.

———•———

For decades, Mina worked methodically and effectively to unravel the mysteries of cancer cell development. Thanks to her background in chemistry, she started (again!) with a radical hypothesis that was initially met with skepticism but is now "here to stay." The concept is rooted in the idea that the extracellular matrix (ECM), a complex meshwork of proteins and carbohydrates made and secreted by cells, in turn influences the shape, biochemistry, and genes that a cell activates, or "turns on." *Half the secret of the cell is outside of the cell!* Mina thought. Mina worked diligently to investigate this concept and has moved others to do the same.

While working, Mina often repeated her favorite Albert Einstein quote to herself: "For an idea that does not at first seem insane, there is no hope." She knew she had to start with unlikely ideas and explore them; otherwise, she would never break new ground in her field.

Mina earned the rank of Distinguished Scientist at Lawrence Berkeley National Laboratory (LBNL). Achieving this title isn't easy for anyone, and it certainly wasn't for Mina. When she first got to LBNL, she was discouraged from seeking a tenure-track position, one of the highest rankings at a university, because Berkeley already had one other woman working as a professor. Mina never let bias deter her, though, even when people were actively discouraging her from exploring new ideas.

She would always remember a time in the 1980s when a renowned scientist took her paper and held it over the wastebasket-- then dropped it in. The scientific community had often resisted or downright rejected her ideas. Mina persevered nonetheless and, with the help of her colleagues and students, turned the world of cancer research upside down by looking at the context in which cancer cells thrive.

Mina has mentored more than ninety successful graduate students and fellows. She has authored hundreds of publications and given more than one hundred "named and distinguished" lectures. Her numerous awards and honors include the AACR Distinguished Lectureship in Breast Cancer Research, two "Innovator Awards" from the U.S. Department of Defense for breast cancer research, the American Cancer Society's Medal of Honor, and the Alexander Bodini Foundation Prize for Scientific Excellence in Medicine. She was recognized for her lifetime contribution to science with "The Mina J. Bissell Award," which was created in her honor by the University of Porto, Portugal. The award is given every two years to a scientist who has transformed perception of a scientific area. The first award was for her pioneering contributions vis-à-vis the role of the microenvironment and context in organ-specific functions and the development of cancer.

WE CAN CHAMPION ONE ANOTHER: A LETTER TO ALL

Dear Readers,

Nothing is only for boys, and nothing is only for girls. The world is deliciously complex. It can be surprising or disappointing, but the future is as bright as the opportunities you seize today.

A rising tide will raise us all, so let's champion one another. Here are a few ways you can ENGAGE with those around you:

- Encourage your fellow classmates to raise their hands and speak up in class.
- Listen patiently and respectfully.
- Invite boys and girls to your labs, classrooms, and clubs.
- Collaborate with those you don't normally work with.
- Support your peers in achieving their goals.
- Take a chance on yourself and others!

Your time is now. What are you waiting for?

Despite these accolades, Mina continues to remind herself and others in the scientific community that "scientific results are not written in stone. Well-designed experiments and unexpected results that lead to new paradigms, and maybe even beget medals and prizes, sooner or later will have to be reexamined as we become wise enough to admit how much more remains to be discovered. I believe deeply that the pull and the beauty of science is its humbling complexity, which leaves no room for arrogance, and that looking at new data with unbiased eyes and awe is the sacred duty of science and scientists." Her early life-lesson of shouldering the burden of proof has stayed with her. She advises her students to remain rigorous in their thinking and experiments. By her own admission, some of her ideas took thirty years to be accepted!

Mina's life's work took her far away from her home country of Iran. When she was just a young college student, she was often homesick for Iran but couldn't afford to travel back to visit her mother and father. After the Iranian Revolution, she became disturbed by what was happening in her country. In Iran, any expression of dissent toward the new revolutionary regime could lead to a jail sentence and, perhaps, even torture and death. She knew that because she had been raised with a strong sense of justice she would not be able to stay silent about the mistreatment she might see in Iran if she went back there.

These days, though, Mina finds herself longing to return to her roots, to the place she was born. Although in the U.S. Iran is often seen as a country that oppresses its people, Mina knows her country is much more complex than that. For example, most students studying engineering, medicine, and architecture at universities across the country are women—and a large percentage of Tehran University's faculty are women.

Mina remembers her childhood growing up in a warm, educated, and forward-thinking family and wishes that people in the U.S. could know more about the vibrant Iranian culture. Iran and its people aren't just about its government's relationship with those who happen to be in the White House!

Mina thinks about the comments often made to her by interviewers or admirers. They tell her that her impressive accomplishments seem at odds with a woman who grew up in the Middle East.

Mina's response for them is: "I believe [it was] precisely because of my background in Iran that I could persist in the era of Mad Men in the 1960s and 1970s, even in the face of some amazingly bad behavior from a number of men in charge."

A P E P TA LK: S TE M NEEDS YOU!

> *"Never be limited by others' limited imagination."*
> *–Mae Jamison, astronaut*

Archimedes Principle.
Avogadro's Law.
Ohm's Law.
Newton's Laws.
Bernoulli Principle.
Pascal's Law.

These principles and laws are all named after the men who discovered them. Their contributions were critical, but where are the women? Hundreds of years later, the shortage of female participation in math and the sciences is jarring!

Did you know that more than one hundred years ago, in the 1890s, close to sixty percent of students studying physics and algebra in the U.S. were girls? Or that in the early 1900s, Marie Curie won *two* Nobel Prizes — one for physics and the other for chemistry?

So why don't we hear more about women studying math and the sciences? One explanation could be that more schools began teaching the classics and home economics instead of science. After World War II, the sciences became more geared toward making weapons, which led to fewer women pursuing science careers. Girls' involvement in the sciences dropped so rapidly that, by the 1950s, the proportion of girls studying physics in the U.S. dropped to twenty percent!

Here are some reasons why…

Lagging interest and confidence
Girls' interest and confidence in Science, Technology, Engineering, Mathematics (STEM) is lower than boys', even though girls' abilities in STEM are similar to their male counterparts. Recently, this gap has become wider as fewer girls express interest in STEM. In 2015, a research study showed that male students were three times more likely to be interested in STEM careers than female students.

Fewer graduates
A disproportionately low number of girls receive STEM degrees in college, even though more than half of college graduates are female. And across the board, women are less likely than men to continue their studies in STEM.

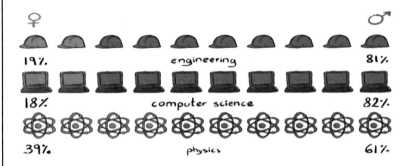

♀   ♂

19%   engineering   81%

18%   computer science   82%

39%   physics   61%

Fewer career options

Females are more likely to make less money in the STEM workforce than their male counterparts, which is an example of the "gender pay gap."

Female researchers who expect to have a family, or who already have children, abandon their work twice as quickly as men, a phenomenon that is sometimes called a "leaky pipeline." This means that more women tend to drop out as they get further along in their careers. Because of this phenomenon, men are employed in STEM occupations at twice the rate of women.

As you can see, the number of women in STEM careers dwindles at every further career stage. Gender representation is not just a matter of balancing the number of men and women who participate in science. **Bringing a diverse perspective to the sciences is essential. It's part of challenging existing ideas, providing new and better solutions, and broadening and deepening our current understandings. If girls don't study STEM, we all lose!**

In the face of unequal opportunities—including the gender pay gap, leaky pipelines, and glass ceilings (barriers to career advancement)—girls still have the power to make a difference, one person at a time.

So, what can *you* do?

First, realize that the world of math and science is vibrant, creative, and inspiring.

Mayim Bialik, the actor who starred in *The Big Bang Theory* and *Blossom*, has a PhD in neuroscience. When she was young, she had a biology teacher who taught her about the cell "as if it was Picasso's most famous painting," Bialik recalls. "I had professors when I was an undergraduate [who] said, 'Why are you here? If you could have the world of acting, why wouldn't you take it?' Being a scientist is as exciting, creative, and interesting as being an artist looking at the sunset. I love that my brain goes to color, wavelength, rotation of the Earth, why the horizon disappears, [and] why it looks different. That's just how I see the world, and I love it. It's like being in love with every aspect of the universe."

Adopt a can-do attitude.
- Be part of the conversation, because you have something to say.
- Challenge yourself, because that's the best way to push your limits.
- Build things and take them apart, because that's the way to learn how things work.
- Test. Fail. Learn. Repeat. Test. Succeed. Learn.

Take action.
- Connect the richness of math and science to your everyday life.
- Join clubs and teams, because math and the sciences are deeper than memorizing equations!
- Do science experiments outside of school, because testing assumptions is the first step to challenging accepted ideas.

Support others.
- Connect with other students who are also interested in math and the sciences.
- Listen and learn from others.

As thirteen-year-old aspiring astronaut Taylor Richardson said, "Science is not a boy's game; it's not a girl's game. It's everyone's game."

Girls can rock STEM, and it starts with you!

درسا درخشانی

DORSA: IN BRIEF

DORSA DERAKHSHANI plays chess like Beyoncé sings. She won championships in Iran and greater Asia—shaking, rattling, and exceeding expectations! Dorsa had mastered playing the two hundred and four squares on a chessboard, but her life proved to have less predictable outcomes. She eventually left Iran, her place of birth, competed briefly in Europe, and then moved to the U.S., where she joined the American chess team, all the while studying biology at university.

DORSA DERAKHSHANI

b. 1998

How does a gifted Iranian chess player find her way to the U.S., where she hopes to become a doctor and an Olympic champion?

The morning that Dorsa woke up from her slumber to compete at her first chess championship was unlike any other morning. For Dorsa, chess was like no other game she had ever played. Sure, like any other competition, it required discipline, self-confidence, and lots of practice, but chess had an unusual flavor. It made Dorsa live totally in the moment. She had to use all of her mental powers. It was exhilarating. On this day, eight-year-old Dorsa would show the world that she would become a formidable contender. She had come a long way from playing chess with her dad on a small magnetic board when she was two.

The mood is still at a tournament. The competition room is as quiet as a final exam room—large, with neatly arranged tables and chairs. Each table has two chairs facing each other.

Sitting on the adult-size chairs at the competition, Dorsa's feet must have been dangling. Each table had a checkered chessboard with opposing black and white pieces and a clock to keep track of the timing of each move made by each player. Each player was assigned to one side of the board. Before entering the chess hall, Dorsa probably knew if she was playing white or black pieces. (As she got older, when she knew with whom she was paired, she would study how they had played in previous competitions.) Opponents playing the white pieces made the first move. If a player noticed an infraction of the rules, she raised her hand for the tournament director to intermediate. At the competitions, each player was paired against a similarly skilled opponent. Rankings were typically based on a player's chess rating.

During Dorsa's first tournament, she, like the other competitors, was focused and played the best chess she knew how. That meant she made the best moves she saw available—not only for her next step, but for the few ahead, as she anticipated what her opponent might do. Skilled chess players studied various openings. Players analyzed and reviewed them as part of their training. The opening laid the groundwork for every game. The more the players practiced, the better they became at recognizing patterns.

There were two possible outcomes—a player won and, therefore, the other one lost, or there was a draw and neither player won.

At the end of this tournament, Dorsa had done very well! She received a giant trophy, almost half the size of her body; she had won the national championship. She smiled into the camera, with her princess dress on, her tiara glittering on her head.

—•—•—•—

Eight years later, by 2014, Dorsa was playing chess for the Iranian Chess Federation. She had progressed rapidly on the team and was now playing in international tournaments. One day, after having already won three Asian championships, she arrived in India for another tournament. Any chess player would be proud of her accomplishments thus far in her career. Since chess had been banned in Iran after the 1979 Revolution and only reinstated in 1988, there weren't many strong chess players in the country and hardly any female players. But that limitation hadn't held Dorsa back.

She was excited to play in the tournament and likely preparing her opening in her head, when she got reprimanded by one of her coaches for what she was wearing. Modestly dressed in a long-sleeved shirt and jeans, Dorsa also had a headscarf, which was mandated by the Iranian team.

What was the matter with her jeans? Dorsa stood her ground. She was following the dress code rules, and she didn't change her clothes when she was asked. She wanted to think about the game she was about to play. The officials on the team seemed more interested in the piece of cloth covering her hair than the brain underneath it.

It was like that time when she was six years old and had to sing a popular Iranian children's song on television. When the producers insisted that she wear a headscarf for the filming, she walked off the show. As a matter of personal choice, some Muslim women don't cover their hair. Dorsa's family was Muslim, and she didn't cover her hair at home. She didn't understand why she had to do so in public. Even back then, Dorsa knew she disagreed with these restrictions, and nothing had changed for her since.

Dorsa eagerly made her way to the room where she would play her first game. Her goal was to become a Woman Grandmaster and an International Master before she turned eighteen years old. That would be a difficult feat, but Dorsa was sure she could do it. She had learned to read when she was just one-and-a-half, and by age two, she had finished the first grade. She had graduated from fourth grade before she turned five. She'd always had an extraordinary mind, and these days it was almost entirely focused on chess.

Dorsa took a seat at the table where she would play her first game. Ever since childhood, she loved mental puzzles, but it wasn't until she tried chess that she knew what her true passion was.

In 2016, Dorsa reached her goal of becoming a Woman Grandmaster and International Master before her eighteenth birthday. She was also the second-highest ranked player for girls under eighteen in the world. (The rating system in chess estimates a player's strength in comparison with other players.) She earned two International Chess Federation (FIDE) titles before finishing high school in Tehran. Now, she had to decide what to do next in her career.

She loved her high school, but she didn't want to stay in Iran much longer. She wanted to pursue opportunities that Iran couldn't offer. Arguing with the officials on her chess team about her style of dress or the habit of speaking her mind was taxing. She decided that after she graduated, she would move to Spain to pursue her studies and receive better chess training.

On the day she left for Spain, Dorsa wept as she hugged her parents. She hated the fact that she would have to leave them behind in order to pursue her dreams.

Her mother insisted that this was the right decision. "For all these years, we've watched you struggle, trying to be yourself. We want you to live somewhere you will be accepted for who you are." Dorsa wiped away her tears. Her mother was right. As much as Dorsa hated to leave home, another part of her was eager for the freedom she knew she would experience abroad.

In Spain, she started playing chess for several European clubs. During that time, she never covered her hair, and no one bothered her about it. No one looked shocked when she said exactly what she was thinking, either. Dorsa's heart and mind were working in unison.

All was going well for Dorsa until, in February 2017, she received notifications from high school friends in Iran, which read, *What did you do? Are you OK? Did they jail you?* At first, Dorsa didn't know what her friends were referring to. Why would anyone want to know if she was okay?

Unbeknownst to her, she had been disqualified from playing for the Iranian Chess Federation. She also couldn't compete at any tournaments in Iran. Dorsa was bewildered. She'd already left the national team. Why would they decide to kick her out of a team she was no longer a part of?

Days before, at the Gibraltar tournament in Spain, Dorsa hadn't covered her hair. She hadn't worn the hijab since she'd arrived in Spain. During the Gibraltar tournament, the only thing on her head had been her trademark headband. Was that why she was being "disqualified"?

Perhaps it was a veiled message. Later, she thought the Iranian Chess Federation possibly had other motives for banning her.

The Federation had been experiencing plenty of problems. The Women's World Chess Championship was being held in Tehran that year, and several important players had boycotted it. Nazí Paikidze-Barnes, a U.S. women's champion, had decided not to go and posted on Instagram: *I think it's unacceptable to host a Women's World Championship in a place where women do not have fundamental rights and are treated as second-class citizens.*

By banning Dorsa, the Iranian Chess Federation was making its position clear. All women had to obey the dress code, or they weren't welcome.

Dorsa was surprised, though, to realize how big the story about her disqualification became. The next day, she saw a newspaper headline that read, *Teenage Iranian Chess Master Banned from National Team for Refusing to Wear a Headscarf.* On international TV, commentators expressed outrage at what had happened.

Dorsa's feelings about the press coverage were mixed. On the one hand, she believed in her right not to have to cover her hair.

However, she was deeply disappointed that Iran was in the news yet again for such a reason. And she noticed how many people were quick to rush to judgment and declare her a victim of the Iranian government—a woman veiled under an authoritarian regime.

This was frustrating. The real story was more complex. She wasn't a victim. She'd been born and raised in a male-dominated theocracy ruling with an iron fist, and yet she had excelled in a world dominated by men. She herself didn't want to wear the hijab, but she knew many women did, for religious, cultural, and personal reasons. The mandate to wear the hijab was oppressive, but it had also been oppressive in the years before the Revolution—when the monarchy said women *couldn't* wear the hijab.

The Iranian dress code presented challenges, especially for foreigners who weren't used to them. But they were part of the nation's laws, and how they changed or didn't change was an issue that gradually evolved within Iran. It couldn't be dictated by outsiders.

Mitra Hejazipour, an Iranian Woman Grandmaster, criticized Paikidze-Barnes's decision to boycott the games. "This is going to be the biggest sporting event women in Iran have ever seen," she said. "We haven't been able to host any world championship in any other sporting fields for women in the past. It's not right to call for a boycott. These games are important for women in Iran. It's an opportunity for us to show our strength." Dorsa hoped that not everyone would boycott the games. She agreed with Mitra inasmuch that the games were an awesome occasion for Iranian chess players to shine. But Dorsa knew all too well what it's like to have the will of others imposed on women.

VEILED BY LIPSTICK OR HIJAB?

 On a hot, sticky day, seeing a nun with a black veil or an Orthodox Jewish woman with a dark tichel (headscarf) doesn't stir the same reaction as seeing a Muslim woman wearing a hijab.

Women covering their hair predates Islam. Married Orthodox Jewish, Hindu, and Catholic women covered their hair long before any Muslim women ever did — and some still do. In Islam, as in many other religions, covering one's hair is a symbol of modesty and privacy. But some may see this particular dress code as a symbol of oppression.

In the East, in places like Iran, wearing the hijab is compulsory. Refusing to wear one results in arrest and corporal punishment. So, the hijab has come to be seen as a tool for dominating women. Some imagine that Muslim women who wear the hijab are trapped and need to be rescued. However, many women, Iranian included, choose to wear the hijab because it is part of their culture — not because a government has criminalized not wearing one. Covering one's hair has been a tradition among Muslim women for hundreds of years!

Conversations about this dress code tend to be highly charged, particularly in the case of Iran. While many young women in Iran do not want the hijab to be obligatory, others defend its cultural and religious merits. In many cases, the hijab has allowed Iranian women to participate more fully in Iranian society, rather than being confined to their homes. It is crucial to have discourse on the topics of mandatory hijab and a women's right to choose. In doing so, it is equally important to refrain from reaching hasty conclusions. Such reactions can have more to do with cultural prejudice than with a deeper understanding of the reasons why women choose — or choose not to — wear the hijab.

Labeling the hijab a tool of political oppression is deceptive. It distracts us from the heart of the matter: challenging governments and institutions when they enact oppressive laws and policies. All cultures embrace a variety of dress codes for numerous reasons, and we have to exercise caution when passing judgment on these norms. We have to appreciate the power of choice in how Muslim women — and all women, for that matter — make decisions about their lives. Some women choose not to wear the hijab for political or personal reasons. If others opt to make different choices, it does not make them less worthy or their actions less relevant. It is the woman's right to determine how to think and behave. Reducing a people to stereotypes begs the question: Are we veiled by lipstick or hijab?

For a while, the pandemonium over Gibraltar dominated the headlines. Then, the furor subsided. By the next spring, Dorsa was playing in tournaments all over Europe. In the summer of 2017, she moved to the U.S. after being accepted to St. Louis University (SLU) — a college with a strong competitive chess team — and earning a chess scholarship. Finally, she would have a stable trainer and a team. Not only that, she could also pursue her dream of becoming a doctor! Dorsa now studies biology and clinical health sciences at SLU.

She loved meeting with her St. Louis team coach, Alejandro Ramirez. He listened sympathetically when she told him about her conflicts with the Iranian chess team, over what she wore and said. Then, he said, "Of course, America is not going to have a problem with that."

Here in the U.S., she would worry less about being silenced for dissent. In 2017, she wrote, "Chess...is pure. It doesn't care about gender, ethnicity, nationality, status, or politics. But too often the countries, organizations, and people who enforce the rules in the world of chess are anything but."

Chess didn't care how old you were or what you wore. It didn't care how much money you had. It was blind to all of that. It cared only about merit.

The world is now Dorsa's oyster. Although her pre-medical track at SLU is demanding and sometimes prevents her from competing in tournaments, she has her heart set on playing at the U.S. Women's Championship and qualifying for the U.S. Olympic team. We can imagine her walking into the tournament, or a hospital operating room, head held high, knowing she will be practical, strategic, and cool under pressure!

CHESS: WHERE ARE THE WOMEN?

NO WOMAN HAS EVER RECEIVED THE TITLE OF WORLD CHESS CHAMPION.

You can count the number of women who have made it to the list of the top one hundred chess players with one hand. As of September 2020, only thirty-seven of the 1,720 Grandmasters were female. That means only two percent of them were women!

Why is there a dearth of women in the upper echelons of chess? Are women less capable? Are they less talented? Do they practice less often than men? Or are there other reasons they do not attain the highest levels of chess mastery?

Chess player Zahir Ahmadov tried to answer these questions. He asked some of the world's best players to explain the dominance of males in their chosen field. He got many answers. Some said women were too emotional. Some said women were physically weaker and became exhausted more easily. Others thought women were too bound by other responsibilities, such as family and chores, to truly excel at chess. And still others said that not enough money was spent on women chess players.

To Ahmadov's dismay, no one mentioned the great disparity in the number of male players versus female players. "… [M]y conclusion was that even female players themselves accepted that men would always be better than them," Ahmadov said. "I was disappointed and wished to hear different answers, like, 'Just wait a few more years and we will overtake men.'"

These attitudes amongst female players are especially troubling, because they are mostly based on stereotypes, not fact. Researcher Merim Bilalić has found that the difference in male and female players' performance comes down, quite simply, to one statistic: Men play chess more often than women. Bilalić knew that, in statistics, highly-rated performers were more likely to come from a bigger group than a smaller group, even if the skill sets of the two groups were the same. So, he and his colleagues took a sample of more than 120,000 German chess players—113,000 men and 7,000 women—and applied a mathematical model to compare the best one hundred players from each group. His conclusion? The larger male group accounted for ninety-six percent of the difference in ability between the two groups.

It seems that the main thing holding women back in chess is that there's not enough of them playing! Recruiting, training, and keeping them will help. But in order for women and girls to succeed, they must keep playing! And, Ahmadov hopes, "…[T]ime will prove these [outdated opinions] wrong, and future generations will witness equal play of women and men."

ANNA: IN BRIEF

ANNA ESKAMANI was raised in Orlando, Florida. In the fifth grade, when she found out that as a result of newly passed legislation she would have to eat lunch separately from her best friend, she petitioned her school to save lunch with her friend. In high school, when she learned in her AP History class that society wasn't equal for everyone, she became inspired to help others. In college, she volunteered at Planned Parenthood and later worked for them. Anna forged ahead despite the many struggles she faced growing up, including losing her mom to cancer when Anna was thirteen. In 2018, Anna became the first American with roots in Iran to be elected as a Florida legislator. She was reelected in 2020.

ANNA ESKAMANI

b. 1990

How do grownups in voting booths across the state of Florida and elected officials in their Tallahassee offices change the way a fifth-grade girl at her Orlando elementary school enjoys lunch?

Anna was at school when she got word that a law had passed in the Florida legislature intended to eventually reduce classroom sizes in Florida's schools. But Bonneville Elementary, Anna's school, was taking action now. School officials were moving students to meet their new requirements—shifting boys and girls from one class to another, switching lunch and recess schedules.

Surely this wouldn't impact Anna's life. Her best friend would remain in her class, and they would still share a lunch period together. Boys and girls strictly adhered to rules about not talking in class, but lunch was special. Most fifth-grade girls liked to chat about today's rudest boy, their weekend plans, and the junk food they would trade for what mom and dad didn't allow at home. Lunch was always tastier with your best friend.

So, when Anna found out that lunch as she knew it would be ending for the remainder of her fifth-grade career, she decided she didn't want to be a spectator, watching from the sidelines.

After school, Anna and Ida, her identical twin, walked home, maybe this time a little faster, eager to find a way to save lunch. At home, there was usually no adult to supervise them after school. Their brother was in high school and wouldn't get home for a while. Mom worked late shifts at K-Mart, and Dad was an electrical engineer on Florida's Space Coast, who also worked at Disney World on the weekends.

Anna's dad had a computer at home for the family to tinker with. Anna sat at his desk, turned on the computer, and typed up a petition on behalf of Bonneville Elementary students to keep their original lunch schedule. She wasn't sure where the idea of petitioning the school officials came from. Maybe she'd seen it on PBS *NewsHour* with her parents or learned about it in school. At any rate, she knew this was a legitimate way to try to get people in authority to take action or change their minds.

If she wanted to be taken seriously, she needed to be thoughtful about how to petition. The document had to make sense. It had to be cogent. It needed a short description of what Anna wanted from the school and the names and signatures of students who agreed with her. She typed it, saved it, pressed print.

The next day, with the petition attached to a clipboard, she began to gather signatures. She had to introduce herself to the students who didn't know her and explain why she was asking for signatures. Would her stomach flutter and her mouth get dry if she had to gather people for a cause she cared about? Anna mustered the courage to ask her friends and strangers for help, because it was something she cared about.

Some of Anna's classmates didn't know what a petition was and Anna had to explain it the best way she could. Some didn't agree with her, but some did and signed her document.

At the end of the day, Anna's paper was full of signatures when she handed it to the school officials. Sometime later, she was informed that the petition had failed. The new lunch schedule remained in effect. But the idea of appealing to greater powers, seeking consensus, and advocating for herself stuck with Anna. For those few days when she believed it would work, Anna had felt on top of the world.

A SEAT AT THE TABLE

"If they don't give you a seat at the table, bring a folding chair." These words were spoken by Shirley Chisholm, the first Black woman elected to the U.S. Congress and the first Black person to run for president. Congresswoman Chisholm knew something about being an outsider breaking barriers. When she spoke about "a seat at the table," she meant being part of a group that makes decisions. In 1968, when she was elected to Congress, Black women did not have much voice in politics. She was determined to change that, even if it wasn't easy.

We've certainly come a long way since 1968, but we still live in a world where some voices are silenced, marginalized, or criminalized.

In February 2018, seventeen people were killed in a Parkland, Florida high school. The assailant brought an assault weapon into the school and gunned down his classmates. While adults scrambled to make sense of it all, the students refused to succumb to idleness. This was urgent!

They used news and social media outlets to broadcast their experience as survivors, and victims of lawmakers' apathy. They assembled rallies, organized boycotts, and invited other youth activists from around the country to join them. They learned how legislators affected gun laws. When they spoke at the mic, they were informed and articulate. Not only did their political journey grab the attention of the world, but they also managed to reverse some politicians' positions on gun rights legislation.

Congresswoman Chisholm and those students in Florida got creative about how they would take part in the decisions that affected them—and you can too! When you face exclusion, resistance, and apathy, respond with inclusion, collaboration, and action. If you are not offered a seat at the table, find another way to get your voice heard.

- Add chairs to their table.
- Stand at their table.
- Protest at their table.
- Boycott their table.
- Assemble your own table.
- Invite others to join you at your table.

This wasn't the only time things didn't move in the direction Anna wanted. During childhood, Anna experienced other disappointments. Like when, days after the terror attacks on September 11th, 2001, a boy who Anna thought was a friend taunted her at the playground. "Are you related to Osama bin Laden?" he asked, smirking. "You're hairy and kinda look like him."

She felt humiliated. It seemed like he was taking pleasure in making her feel like an outsider. Was he trying to tell her she didn't belong in America? Why was he comparing her, an eleven-year-old girl, to a terrorist? Was he implying that she was one? His comments hurt and shamed her. Anna felt ugly and unwelcomed. She clenched her fists. Her Baba had told her to stay out of trouble and not to draw attention to herself, but that boy's words made her want to start a fight.

Anna wanted to talk to her mother about the incident, but it didn't seem pressing enough. When Anna was eight, her mother had been diagnosed with colon cancer, and things had recently taken a turn for the worse. The playground episode seemed trivial — maybe not worth talking about.

As the years passed, Anna's mother's treatments resulted in awful side effects. One day, Anna found her mom throwing up in the bathroom. Someone needed to clean up the mess. As Anna wiped up the bathroom, her mother stood looking into the mirror. "Anna *jan*, I look so ugly." She spoke in Farsi, as she always did to her children. "Look at how thin I am."

Anna looked at her mother's yellowed skin — she had jaundice brought on by the cancer. Even the whites of her almond-shaped eyes had yellowed.

What was the right response at that moment? What could she say to her sick mom? Sometimes, it was easier to think about how to sanitize the bathroom instead.

Anna's mother pressed her hands to her hair and mused that at least her hair was still thick. Iranian women were known for their lustrous locks.

Ajax, the cleaning agent, could do the trick. Anna said nothing. She cleaned the toilet, and not for the last time. Her mother often felt insecure about herself. First it was her appearance, then it was the house. If it wasn't clean enough, she worried that her husband would leave her. Anna felt sad for her mother. She was lovely and intelligent—why didn't she feel that she was worth more? Anna wondered if her mom had been born in the wrong place at the wrong time. If she'd been born later, in a different country, maybe she would have more confidence in herself.

But maybe not. Anna wasn't sure of anything herself. Her body was now changing in ways she didn't understand. At school, all the girls took a life skills course and the teacher handed out pads and tampons for them to bring home. Anna tucked them away in her backpack, but she still wasn't sure what to do when her period started. She didn't want to talk to her mom about it. For as long as she could remember, the idea of puberty embarrassed Anna. Now that her breasts were developing, she found herself covering her chest all the time, keeping her arms folded across it whenever she could.

Anna's mom finally sat down with Anna and Ida in their bedroom.

"Girls, we have to talk about your changing bodies," she said.

"Okay, Mom, maybe later," Anna said quickly. "We'll have time to talk about it later."

Later must have felt safer. From the boy who made fun of her to her ailing mother, menstruation was like throwing a monkey wrench into the mix. Anna didn't like to think about getting her period. She had a superstition that when she got her period, her mom would die. She didn't want to get older, and she didn't want her mom to get any sicker.

But Anna couldn't stop the passage of time, or the progression of her mom's illness. When she was thirteen years old, her mother passed away. At the memorial service, Anna stood up in front of her friends and family and said she wanted to be just like her mother when she grew up, compassionate, strong, and optimistic. She remembered how hard her mother had worked at a series of minimum-wage jobs, at the donut shop where she and Anna's dad— immigrants to the U.S. from Iran—first met, at a fast-food restaurant, and at the K-Mart where she worked long hours. Anna teared up as she remembered helping her mom clean shelves and fold clothes at work. She missed her mother so much already. How would she ever get by without her?

———————

Years later, when Anna graduated from college and began working for an organization called Planned Parenthood, she recalled how difficult it had been for her after her mother died. Her father had begun a job that required him to travel extensively. Anna didn't know to whom she could turn when she had questions about her changing body. And even if her dad had been around, it wasn't normal for an Iranian girl to seek her dad's guidance on puberty.

In 2008, when Anna was eighteen and needed to learn more about reproductive health and family planning, she'd sought out Planned Parenthood. That organization taught her about menstruation, abstinence, contraceptives, and sexually transmitted infections. She was grateful that there was a place to help her better understand how a girl becomes a woman, and what a woman needs to know to best take care of herself.

That experience was one of the reasons Anna was so passionate about working for Planned Parenthood. Sure, in the U.S. women have the right to vote, own property, or work, but it hadn't always been that way, and things could still be fairer and just for them. In Mr. Morris' high school AP Government class, she had become more interested in women's rights. His class discussions helped her understand how society wasn't equal for everyone, that too many lived with limited prospects to thrive; some were treated as "others" because of what they looked like. In her own family, she witnessed how some immigrants struggled. In the 1970s, her parents emigrated to the U.S. from Iran, and Anna had seen firsthand their lack of access to basic needs that many of her classmates took for granted, like reliable healthcare and a better quality of life. Even though her parents worked unfalteringly at multiple jobs, they couldn't attain the kind of life they wanted for themselves and their children. In Mr. Morris' class, Anna truly felt inspired. He'd doused the flames from Anna's elementary school days. His class prompted Anna to want to do something to change the way things worked in the U.S.

Now that Anna worked at Planned Parenthood, this time as an advocate and not a patient seeking knowledge about her reproductive health, she had a chance to be part of that change. She loved the work—it allowed her to use all the knowledge she gained as a political science and women's studies major in college. She could see that she was making a difference in her community. Still, she wanted to do even more.

Anna looked at what state legislators were doing in Florida and thought she could do better. She cared about her community and advocated for it. Plus, through her work with Planned Parenthood and other community-based organizations, she knew the political landscape of her district. She could become a government representative one day.

In 2017, just two months after she turned twenty-seven, Anna announced her candidacy for the Florida House of Representatives, District 47. This district is home to Pulse Nightclub, which on June 12th, 2016, became the scene of the second-worst mass shooting by a single perpetrator in U.S. history. Forty-nine people were killed, and fifty-three were injured.

When she first began running for office, Anna was filled with excitement and energy. But running for office turned out to be more tiring and brutal than she'd expected. Everything she'd ever said or done was dissected under a microscopic lens. People talked about her, and some criticized her. Her political opponent dug up footage of her speaking during a protest at the 2017 Women's March in Washington, D.C. Because she'd used curse words during her speech, he called her "vulgar" and "extremely partisan."

He advertised an image of himself—quiet, seated with a conventional, white middle-class family consisting of a husband, wife, and two children—juxtaposed against an unflattering image of Anna as a defiant, unruly woman, with prominent features and wavy dark hair. Online, people expressed hostility toward her because of her ethnicity. It was cruel. It served as a reminder of her playground days when she was sneered at and likened to a grown man responsible for terrorizing the U.S. and killing thousands of people.

Anna felt the strain of running for office. It was a lonely experience to be a woman of color and a target of bigotry. But she also felt motivated by her mission. People were counting on her. Many who worked on her campaign were getting involved in the political process for the first time. An elementary-school student who had seen Anna campaign became encouraged by her and ran for the student council at her school—and won! Through it all, Anna remembered that she was influencing her community and encouraging students, who had been just like her in elementary school, to become involved in the political process. So, she persevered.

She raised $12,000 on her first day of fundraising, and eventually, her campaign raised more than half a million dollars—more than twice the amount her opponent raised. She began to receive more endorsements—even one from President Barack Obama. But one of the first and most important endorsements was the one she received from her father.

On November 6th, 2018, Anna won the election, receiving fifty-seven percent of the vote. She was elated. She'd become the first woman of Iranian descent to win a seat in the Florida House of Representatives.

The heavy weight of her responsibility was not lost on Anna. After she was elected, Iranians immediately began calling her office and asking for help with issues like travel visas, the Muslim travel ban, and being separated from their loved ones overseas. However, as exhausting as it was to be an elected official, Anna also found it energizing. "This is mission-driven work, and this is fighting for people," she said. That's why Floridians had voted for her!

In November 2018, we witnessed a surge of women of color being elected to public office in the U.S. Here are two trailblazers with roots in Iran.

Anna Kaplan
- First Iranian-American woman to be elected to the New York State Legislature
- Born to a Jewish family in Tabriz, Iran
- Left Iran when she was thirteen and was eventually granted asylum in the U.S.
- Grew up in New York, where she attended college and law school
- Began her political career serving as a councilwoman on her town board

Anna says: "It's the most American of stories, but the story's beginning as a frightened, powerless minority animates everything I do. And my undying gratitude to this great country for taking me in during my most desperate hour is what compels me to public service."

Zahra Karinshak
- First Iranian-American woman to be elected to the Georgia State Legislature
- Military veteran, former federal prosecutor, daughter of an immigrant
- Grew up in poverty in rural Georgia with an Iranian father and American mother
- Attended the U.S. Air Force Academy
- Recognized by her peers as a Top 100 Georgia Super Lawyer

Zahra says: "My two daughters inspired me to run. During the 2016 election, they observed that 'no one is being kind to each other, and you, mom, have to do something to bring us together.' They are right. Politics has turned too divisive, and partisanship runs deep. I am running to bridge the political divide and to restore trust, ethics, and civility back into our public discourse. In the State Senate, I will work with all my constituents — Democrat, Republican, and otherwise — to move our state forward."

When Anna remembers how often she felt different growing up, she's reminded of her election. She hopes that her success will lead others to become involved in their communities. She learned very early on that those elected to public office impact our lives daily, in more ways than we can count with one hand. And the memories of her mother — her work ethic, her deep dedication to her family, and the struggles she endured — continue to propel Anna to fight for the voiceless, the powerless, and the stateless.

ACT(IVISM) BEFORE YOUR RIGHTS
BECOME A CRIME

"I had two options. One was to remain silent and wait to be killed, and the second was to speak up and be killed. I chose the second option. I decided to speak up."

Malala Yousafzai, a Pakistani education activist and the youngest Nobel Laureate, spoke these words during her acceptance speech for the Nobel Peace Prize. Malala was fifteen years old when a Taliban gunman walked onto her school bus, asked for her, pointed a gun, and shot her in the head. She survived.

But that gunman had wanted her dead. Girls under the Taliban regime were not allowed to go to school, and Malala's efforts to reopen the schools had led to a global outcry. When Malala was twelve, she began blogging for the BBC, was featured in a documentary by *The New York Times*, and became known for publicly advocating for female education. These political acts nearly cost Malala her life.

Malala's mission to stand up for her rights is not unique. She is part of a group of everyday young people who advocate for themselves, their neighbors, and their communities.

Ahed Tamimi, a Palestinian, was sixteen when she was arrested for slapping an Israeli soldier. She served eight months in an Israeli prison, where many of her family members had also served time. Upon her release from prison, she became a symbol of the hundreds of detained Palestinian minors in Israeli prisons, many of whom, like Ahed, have resisted Israel's occupation of Palestinian territories and yearn for peaceful childhoods.

Other young people are passionately taking action on behalf of the environment. Xiuhtezcatl Roske-Martinez, an indigenous youth activist rooted in Aztec tradition, began his advocacy work on protecting the environment when he was just six years old. He spoke to world leaders at the United Nations when he was only fifteen, but now he prefers performing in front of crowds at music festivals! Today, he is a lead plaintiff in a case against the U.S. government for failing to protect the environment for future generations.

There's also Bana Alabed, who spread the news about the heavy toll the Syrian civil war had taken on her and her people when she was only seven years old. In 2017, she published a book, *Dear World: A Syrian Girl's Story of War and Plea for Peace*, which highlighted the cruelties of war, her displacement as a refugee, and the humanity we all share. In the book, Bana helps readers realize how this sort of devastation can impact the rest of people's lives. Her mother, remorseful because she couldn't shield her daughter from witnessing the ugliness of war, asked Bana, "Are there two versions of you--the one you would have been if you had grown up in peace, and the girl you are now, shaped by war?"

JASMIN: IN BRIEF

JASMIN MOGHBELI was born in Germany to Iranian parents and moved to the U.S. when she was very young. She grew up in Long Island, New York. Her love of math and physics made her longing to become an astronaut even more inspiring. After attending college at Massachusetts Institute of Technology (MIT), she joined the U.S. Marines and flew an attack helicopter in combat zones. In 2017, she joined NASA's exceptional team of astronauts.

JASMIN MOGHBELI

b. 1983

How did a sixth-grade school presentation on a Soviet cosmonaut spark a young girl's desire to become an astronaut?

Jasmin, a gawky sixth grader with dark, curly tresses, adored math and science. So, when it came time to prepare a report on a person she admired, she chose Valentina Tereshkova, a Soviet cosmonaut who was also the first woman to go into space. Jasmin wanted to dress as Valentina to deliver it.

She and her mom worked diligently to create a spacesuit made from an oversized, white windbreaker and a helmet made from a plastic container and piece of white cloth.

This project was important to Jasmin. She loved math and science, so the thought of someone combining their knowledge of those subjects to go on a great space adventure was exhilarating. Valentina had done what no woman — and very few men — had done before. She had gone into space, blazing a trail and creating new opportunities for others. Valentina was truly unique.

Jasmin knew something about standing out. She was born in Germany to Iranian parents who had left there after the 1979 Revolution and converted from Islam to Lutheranism, a branch of Christianity. When Jasmin was just a baby, her family moved again, this time to New York, where she grew up in a suburb outside of New York City. She celebrated becoming an American citizen with homemade brownies shared with her second-grade classmates.

Jasmin stood out from her classmates, not just because of her heritage but also because of her keen mind and interest in combining art and math. Her parents' backgrounds in architecture encouraged Jasmin to find solutions to mathematical questions through good design.

As Jasmin and her mother labored over her spacesuit costume, Jasmin wondered if one day she would have her own spacesuit, this time made by NASA. One day, she hoped she would get to fly into space, like Valentina had.

Jasmin's report on Valentina marked the beginning of her passion for flying. In high school, she attended the Advanced Space Academy, a camp in Alabama. There, kids took part in astronaut simulation exercises, engineering challenges, and team-building activities. At camp, Jasmin loved wearing the royal-blue flight suit that was a replica of the ones NASA astronauts wore. When it was finally time to return home from camp, she tucked the flight suit into her bag and planned to wear it for Halloween that year.

But becoming an astronaut would require far more than the fun challenges Jasmin participated in at camp. Astronauts had to study many subjects, including biology, physics, astronomy, computer science, and math. So, when Jasmin graduated from high school, she headed to college at the world-renowned MIT to study aerospace engineering and information technology.

———

At MIT, Jasmin — now a tall, lean young woman — attended a campus career fair. She had really enjoyed her first few years at MIT, but becoming an astronaut still seemed like a faraway dream. Still, she'd been having the time of her life in college, playing varsity basketball, lacrosse, and volleyball, all while taking challenging classes in math and science. She stopped at the table with the Marine Corps banner hanging above it and listened to the recruiter describe the training program for pilots. She was eager to learn more. Getting qualified as a pilot could help her to qualify as an astronaut! Feeling encouraged, she decided to sign up.

Many months later, just before starting flight school, Jasmin watched a space shuttle launch at night. She and her friends sat and watched the burst of light underneath the rocket as it hurtled toward space. Sunita Williams was on that flight. Sunita was a female astronaut who had trained as a Navy helicopter pilot. Now, Jasmin was following in Sunita's footsteps.

While serving with the Marines, Jasmin continued with her studies and earned a master's degree in aerospace engineering from the Naval Postgraduate School. She also graduated from the distinguished U.S. Navy Test Pilot School with 1,600 hours of flight time under her belt and experience flying combat missions in Afghanistan.

Soon after learning to fly helicopters, Jasmin was selected to fly Cobras, the military's attack helicopters. Her nickname, "Jaws," was imprinted on the chopper she flew. As she buckled herself into the cockpit, she realized how thankful she was that she'd become a Marine. The experience helped her grow as person. While once she had been terrified of public speaking, now she regularly flew her Cobra into dangerous war zones and afterwards stood up in front of her boss and other senior colleagues to give briefings on her missions.

When Jasmin finished her posting in Afghanistan, she was sent to Arizona, where she was tasked with giving the final thumbs-up or thumbs-down to new flight devices and systems before they were sent to the fleet. Although this job didn't involve flying, Jasmin still enjoyed it. She was learning so much about how physical and psychological information helped with the design of new devices and systems — this was called human-factors engineering, which helped NASA design new spacecraft to send people into space.

In 2013, NASA put out a call for astronaut applicants, but Jasmin hesitated to apply. At that time, she wasn't sure her application would be strong enough. She wasn't yet a senior pilot and she didn't have a graduate degree. So, she stayed on top of the application timeline, since NASA tends to accept applications every few years. To her surprise, the next time NASA issued a call for applicants was only two years later, in 2015. This time, Jasmin jumped at the chance and applied.

The application process was excruciating. First, she had to submit a resume with five references and a summary of her aeronautical experience. After that, she had to wait for NASA to narrow down its list of applicants from 18,000 to just five hundred individuals. Jasmin waited nervously to find out whether she made the first cut. When she found out she had, it was one of the most exhilarating days of her life.

Then, she made it to a narrowed-down pool of one hundred and twenty candidates. She dropped everything and flew to Johnson Space Station in Texas for her interviews. The next three days were both thrilling and grueling, as she and nine other candidates completed teamwork exercises and were interviewed in front of the Astronaut Selection Board. Jasmin was humbled and impressed by the outstanding quality of the other contenders, which made her even more focused and determined to become an astronaut. In the second-round interviews, she met with current astronauts, engineers, medical staff, and other behind-the-scenes teams. Finally, NASA selected the crew members—five women and eight men. Jasmin was one of them!

When she received the congratulatory call from NASA, she was opening a door to a hotel room where she was staying. She was so ecstatic that she nearly dropped the phone. Afterwards, with trembling hands, she dialed her parents, who were eating at a pizza parlor. Her father cried tears of joy and became so emotional that he couldn't drive back home. Jasmin's mother, although also very pleased for her daughter, was worried. "Can you be an astronaut, but just not go to space?" she said.

But going to space was the whole point! Soaring into the unknown of deep space had been Jasmin's dream for a long time. She knew the first manned flights to Mars were projected for some time in the 2030s, and as an astronaut, she could potentially take part in them.

This was a life-changing moment. Jasmin was among an awe-inspiring group of new colleagues. The selected crew had incredible qualifications. Five held doctorate degrees, seven were current or former military officers, one was a former Navy Seal and emergency physician, two had experience in NASA's robotic exploration programs, and one worked on NASA's *Curiosity* Mars rover at the Jet Propulsion Laboratory in California.

One of the reasons Jasmin may have been selected over other candidates was because she had experience living and working in harsh environments, which she gained during her missions in Afghanistan. Astronauts needed that kind of understanding to adjust to long-term space flights, which involved staying in space for more than six months on the ISS or even exploring deep space. Round-trip travel to Mars, for instance, was a three-year proposition!

Jasmin's mind raced ahead to when she would take her first flight into space. She'd get to eat space food — like space steak! And she wouldn't be fazed by the cramped environment in the space shuttle. In the Marines, when she was deployed on a Navy ship, she'd gotten used to living in tight spaces. She remembered how she curled up in her small bunk on the ship.

One of the things she was most psyched about was getting into the neutral buoyancy lab to train for space walks. The neutral buoyancy lab was where the astronaut candidates got in a big pool and practiced walking in a life-size mockup of the ISS. For the astronauts, training in the pool simulated the weightlessness of space.

LIFE ON THE INTERNATIONAL SPACE STATION

What object floats about two hundred and fifty miles above Earth's surface, sleeps about ten people in little capsule-like beds, has magnificent views of home, and is accessible without a passport?

The International Space Station (ISS)!

The ISS is one of humanity's most ambitious technological and political collaborations. It belongs to the U.S., Canada, Japan, Russia, and eleven member states of the European Space Agency.

It is the size of an American football field and weighs more than four hundred tons. Its image reminds some of a floating prefabricated home. The canister and sphere-like shapes are modules that house the astronauts, and the wide, wing-like panels are used to collect sunlight and convert that energy into electricity. Once every ninety-two minutes, at roughly 17,000 miles an hour, the ISS orbits the Earth—so, in twenty-four hours, it circles the Earth sixteen times. Using the ISS Tracker on the European Space Agency website, you can locate its flight path and see it as it passes over your home.

An astronaut's life in this spacecraft is both similar to and different from ours here on Earth. Sure, the astronauts have many routines similar to yours—they eat, sleep, work, read, and exercise—but how they accomplish those things is unique. For starters, there's no gravity on the space station, so everything must be duct-taped, clipped, Velcro-ed, or attached in some other form to a secure, non-moving surface. That means when astronauts eat, brush their teeth, or even go to the bathroom, they have to watch out—things can fly everywhere!

With zero gravity also comes the loss of bone density and muscle mass, so the astronauts have to be in excellent physical condition before they go to the ISS, and they have to continue a rigorous exercise program, like weight-lifting, while in space. The astronauts' food often comes in the form of dehydrated meals to which they add water, but some foods are ready to be heated from cans. Fresh fruits and vegetables are a rare treat; they arrive periodically and have to be consumed quickly. The astronauts do not eat bread, because breadcrumbs flying around in zero gravity make a big mess—tortillas are preferable because they are tidier to consume.

An important part of astronauts' responsibilities is performing experiments in the zero-gravity labs. Before arriving on the ISS for their missions, astronauts extensively study the experiments they will conduct in space. The ISS has five laboratory modules. The U.S., the European Union, and Japan each have a dedicated module, and Russia has two mini-modules. At any time, there are multiple experiments happening in a variety of disciplines on the space station. You can visit NASA's Space Station and Technology site to learn more about their experiments in biology, Earth science, space science, human research, technology, and more.

The most unforgettable (but also most infrequent) activity an astronaut undertakes is the "spacewalk." When astronauts take a walk on the space station, they must wear three-hundred-pound space suits, which take four hours to put on. This weightless-in-space suit is equipped with—among other things—heating and cooling systems and an internal computer that informs the astronaut how the suit is functioning. For example, it tells the astronaut if there is too much oxygen or carbon dioxide in the suit. Spacewalks happen when parts of the space station need to be fixed, and astronauts train intensely for them.

"Space exploration [is] … a reminder of the good and the glorious that we can achieve if we set our minds to it. … The exploration of the solar system is one of the signature enterprises of our time. We should be reveling in it. It belongs to us."

–Carolyn Porco, planetary scientist

All that and more was ahead of her in the next two years of training. She would undergo survival training, master robotics, learn about the ISS, and study Russian so she could communicate with Russian cosmonauts on the ISS. (Although English is the working language of the ISS, as of the writing of this book, the entire crew is delivered to the station by *Soyuz*, a Russian ship. The commander of *Soyuz* is always Russian, and Mission Control communicates only in Russian to everyone in the *Soyuz*.) And once she completed her training, she would be assigned technical duties in the Astronaut Office while she awaited a flight assignment.

In June of 2017, Jasmin wore her NASA uniform (the real one!) and walked onto a stage for the announcement of NASA's new class of astronauts. As she approached her seat in the second row, she heard a little girl in the audience whisper, "Look, mommies can be astronauts too!" In that moment, Jasmin was not only proud of all she had achieved to be able to walk onto that stage, but also pleased to set an example for others — as a woman, an athlete, an immigrant, a Marine, and now, an astronaut.

Jasmin was overjoyed by her selection as an astronaut, but she was also disturbed by the political climate in America. Just before her appointment as an astronaut, President Trump had enacted a travel ban aimed at six predominantly Muslim countries, one of which was Iran. It upset Jasmin to see disapproval and distrust directed toward people who, like her, came from Iran and other Middle Eastern countries.

In the face of these troubling sentiments, it was difficult to stay silent. Jasmin wrote on her Facebook page, *Just remember, when I'm successful from all my hard work, that I was born in Germany (that's where Nazis come from) and my parents are both from Iran (that's where terrorists come from).*

Jasmin wears her Iranian heritage with pride. She celebrates Nowruz (the secular Iranian new year), and wants other immigrants like her to have pride in their roots. The bridges we build make us into the best versions of ourselves — not just as individuals, but as communities and nations. Immigrants have been and continue to be a critical part of the American tapestry.

Jasmin's roots are in Iran. She is also honored to be an American Marine, an astronaut, and a patriot. She's taken advantage of the vast opportunities the U.S. has afforded her as an immigrant. The U.S. also shines better because she is one of its proud citizens! Jasmin has come so far from her sixth-grade days—when she dressed as a Russian cosmonaut—and she will go so much farther!

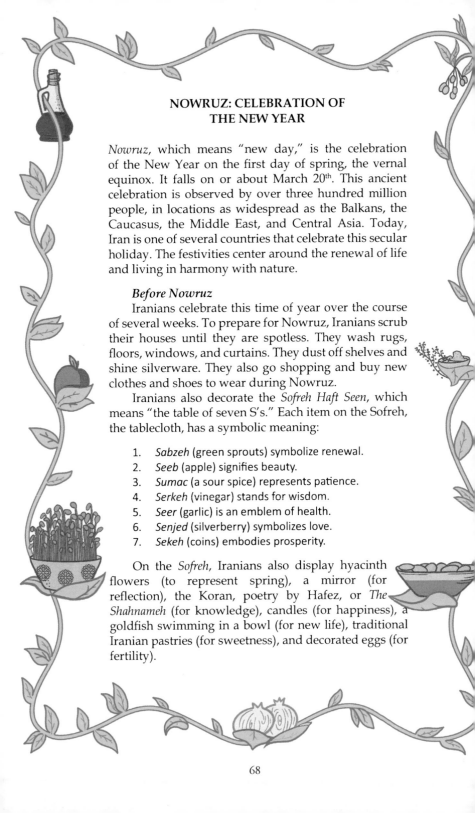

NOWRUZ: CELEBRATION OF
THE NEW YEAR

Nowruz, which means "new day," is the celebration of the New Year on the first day of spring, the vernal equinox. It falls on or about March 20th. This ancient celebration is observed by over three hundred million people, in locations as widespread as the Balkans, the Caucasus, the Middle East, and Central Asia. Today, Iran is one of several countries that celebrate this secular holiday. The festivities center around the renewal of life and living in harmony with nature.

Before Nowruz

Iranians celebrate this time of year over the course of several weeks. To prepare for Nowruz, Iranians scrub their houses until they are spotless. They wash rugs, floors, windows, and curtains. They dust off shelves and shine silverware. They also go shopping and buy new clothes and shoes to wear during Nowruz.

Iranians also decorate the *Sofreh Haft Seen*, which means "the table of seven S's." Each item on the Sofreh, the tablecloth, has a symbolic meaning:

1. *Sabzeh* (green sprouts) symbolize renewal.
2. *Seeb* (apple) signifies beauty.
3. *Sumac* (a sour spice) represents patience.
4. *Serkeh* (vinegar) stands for wisdom.
5. *Seer* (garlic) is an emblem of health.
6. *Senjed* (silverberry) symbolizes love.
7. *Sekeh* (coins) embodies prosperity.

On the *Sofreh*, Iranians also display hyacinth flowers (to represent spring), a mirror (for reflection), the Koran, poetry by Hafez, or *The Shahnameh* (for knowledge), candles (for happiness), a goldfish swimming in a bowl (for new life), traditional Iranian pastries (for sweetness), and decorated eggs (for fertility).

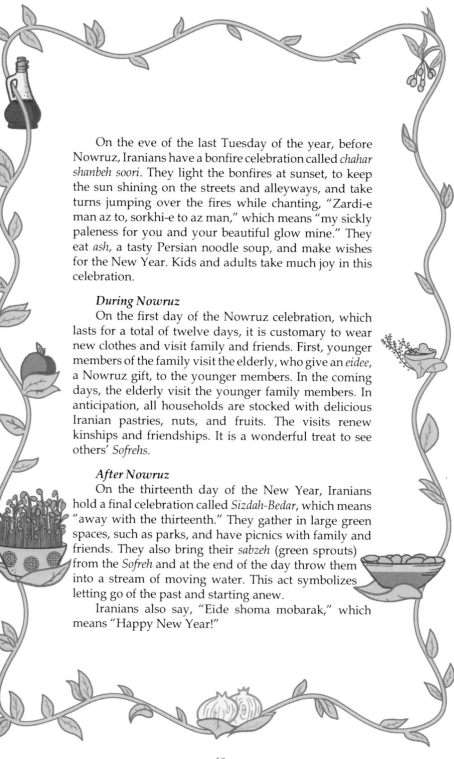

On the eve of the last Tuesday of the year, before Nowruz, Iranians have a bonfire celebration called *chahar shanbeh soori*. They light the bonfires at sunset, to keep the sun shining on the streets and alleyways, and take turns jumping over the fires while chanting, "Zardi-e man az to, sorkhi-e to az man," which means "my sickly paleness for you and your beautiful glow mine." They eat *ash*, a tasty Persian noodle soup, and make wishes for the New Year. Kids and adults take much joy in this celebration.

During Nowruz

On the first day of the Nowruz celebration, which lasts for a total of twelve days, it is customary to wear new clothes and visit family and friends. First, younger members of the family visit the elderly, who give an *eidee*, a Nowruz gift, to the younger members. In the coming days, the elderly visit the younger family members. In anticipation, all households are stocked with delicious Iranian pastries, nuts, and fruits. The visits renew kinships and friendships. It is a wonderful treat to see others' *Sofrehs*.

After Nowruz

On the thirteenth day of the New Year, Iranians hold a final celebration called *Sizdah-Bedar*, which means "away with the thirteenth." They gather in large green spaces, such as parks, and have picnics with family and friends. They also bring their *sabzeh* (green sprouts) from the *Sofreh* and at the end of the day throw them into a stream of moving water. This act symbolizes letting go of the past and starting anew.

Iranians also say, "Eide shoma mobarak," which means "Happy New Year!"

WHAT GOES UP ALSO COMES DOWN:
SPACE STUDIES BENEFIT US ALL

"That's one small step for a man, one giant leap for mankind."

— Neil Armstrong

Studying space is an international enterprise. NASA's work helps us look at galaxies far away while also improving the quality of our lives here on Earth. Often, we don't realize how these studies make our lives better. But if you dig around, you can see that the exploration of space has impacted our daily lives in more ways than you might imagine. For instance, NASA researchers and engineers report more than 1,600 new inventions every year. They then publish the results of their work, which encourages governments and private businesses to make the discoveries available for public use.

Since 1976, NASA has profiled its technological breakthroughs in a publication called *Spinoff*, which chronicles many of the space inventions that have made it to Earth for our use. One such invention is FINDER, a tool that NASA originally developed to study small movements in space. The government had approached NASA for help creating a detection instrument that could locate troops still alive on a battlefield. NASA then developed a prototype and partnered with R4 Incorporated, a private company, to make a tool that could rescue people in the midst of mass devastation. In 2015, when an enormous earthquake rocked Kathmandu, Nepal, and killed more than 8,500 people, rescue workers used FINDER to search for victims buried under the rubble. With the help of FINDER, rescue crews located four men trapped beneath the debris of fallen buildings.

R4 later made improvements to FINDER, reducing the time the technology took to find a heartbeat, and mounted FINDER on drones in areas where the devastation was too intense for rescuers to go.

Another NASA invention became the basis for a new exercise regime. NASA's research into resistance training began because astronauts who spent extended amounts of time in space were losing muscle mass and bone density. Astronauts became so weak after long stints in space that they had to be helped off the space shuttle when they returned to Earth. In 1996, NASA Astronaut Shannon Lucid spent hundreds of hours exercising on the Russian Space Station, Mir, so she could avoid losing strength. However, when she returned to Earth after her one hundred and eighty-eight day stay (the longest ever for any woman), she was still weak.

NASA medical officers realized they needed to come up with a better plan for astronauts. That's when NASA scientists developed the "first resistive exercise hardware that anyone had ever built for space flight." Since then, resistance training — where individuals build strength without using weights — has become an extremely popular and effective workout routine here on Earth.

Here are some other technologies first developed for space studies that have made their way to your doctor's office, your home, and even your food.

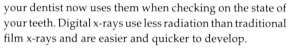

Digital x-rays were first developed by NASA, but

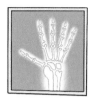

your dentist now uses them when checking on the state of your teeth. Digital x-rays use less radiation than traditional film x-rays and are easier and quicker to develop.

Life support technology, which is widely used in intensive care units today, was originally used to track the physiological status of astronauts on Project Mercury, the first U.S. human space-flight program.

At-home blood pressure kits were originally designed to assess how astronauts' blood pressure changed when they were in space.

Handheld vacuum cleaners are based on a technology that the Apollo astronauts used to drill and gather rock samples on the Moon.

Freeze-dried food was invented by NASA researchers to help astronauts get proper nutrition while on their missions.

While exploring the use of algae, NASA scientists discovered DHA and ARA, two fatty acids produced naturally in human milk that help underdeveloped babies grow. This discovery helped manufacturers improve baby formula.

SNAPSHOTS

KIMIA ALIZADEH

b. 1998

KIMIA ALIZADEH, a taekwondoka and the sole Iranian Olympic medalist since Iran entered the games in 1948, defected to Germany in 2020.

In 2016, she won a bronze medal representing Iran at the summer Olympics in Rio de Janeiro. After her victory, she said, "I am so happy for Iranian girls. I hope at the next Olympics we get gold."

A darling of the Iranian regime and the people of Iran, she was publicly lauded by Hassan Rouhani when he was campaigning to become president. Her medals encouraged other girls and women who wanted to play sports. But her course wasn't easy.

Her modest upbringing meant scarce resources when she was growing up. Kimia's mother was a housewife and her dad sewed embroidery, including the one on her uniform belt. Relentless hours of practice and long commutes to school inescapably led to a late start on her schoolwork. Kimia even had to repeat a grade. She suffered from several sports-related injuries, some of which required surgery.

A year after her Olympic win, she earned a silver medal at the World Taekwondo Championships. In 2019, the BBC listed Kimia as one of the top one hundred inspiring and influential women from around the world!

Abandoning Iran left her with a heavy heart. When she defected, her first post on social media questioned whether she was saying goodbye or sending condolences to her home country.

She had hoped to compete in the 2020 Olympics in Japan, on either Germany's team or the International Olympic Committee's refugee team. Alas, the 2020 Olympics were canceled because of the COVID-19 global pandemic. No matter where she competes, Kimia wrote, "This decision [to defect] is even harder than winning the Olympic gold, but I remain the daughter of Iran wherever I am."

SHIRIN EBADI

b. 1947

SHIRIN EBADI is the first woman from the Islamic world to receive the Nobel Peace Prize. At the award ceremony, in 2003, the Chairman read a quote by Saadi, a thirteenth-century Persian poet: "He who is indifferent to the suffering of others is a traitor to that which is truly human." He said that Shirin and the Iranian people, in the tradition of centuries-old Persian poets, personified both "guide and bridge-builder." He continued, "You are young in spirit. You possess great gifts. You have a warm heart. You are brave. We admire your efforts. The world needs you."

Shirin's birthplace, Hamedan, is one of Iran's oldest cities. Visitors, by the thousands, are drawn to its sprawling mountains and historic monuments.

Before the 1979 Revolution, Shirin was one of the first female judges in Iran. After the revolution, all female judges were dismissed, so Shirin authored books, raised her daughters, and eventually opened a private law practice. Her advocacy work ultimately led to her many arrests and death threats.

From exile, Shirin has continued to promote the rights of women and children. In her speech at the gathering of women Nobel Peace Prize laureates in The Hague, she said, "I demand that the United Nations, encourage all countries to reduce their military budgets and use it for the education and welfare of the people. And I want to ask the United States and the Western world to throw books at people. You will see that we will have a better world in the future."

When asked what advice she would give young people, she said, "This is your life...It's not enough just to vote—after that you must see if those you voted for [came] through....Democracy is like a flower. You must give it water and sun daily. Democracy needs daily maintenance."

Momentous words for all of us, no matter where we live!

MELODY EHSANI
b. 1980

MELODY EHSANI was born in Los Angeles, to an Iranian family who practiced the Bahá'í faith. She spoke Farsi at home, listened to hip-hop, and collected sneakers. With the death of her father when she was ten, creative pursuits took a back seat. It wasn't until she read the words of Bahá'u'lláh, the founder of the Bahá'í faith — "Regard man as a mine, rich in gems of inestimable value" — in her 20s that she found her way. She thought, *Oooh, we all have these gems of inestimable value, but it is our responsibility to mine those gems!* She "set off on a mission of mining [her] own gems."

She took art classes and completed an internship with a sneaker company. Then, she moved to China for five months, to find a factory that would manufacture her shoe designs. When she returned to the U.S., she had her first shoe collection!

Back in Los Angeles, Melody became the first woman to open a store on Fairfax Avenue, the streetwear hub known for its boys' club stores. Melody expanded into jewelry design, and celebrities like Erykah Badu started wearing Melody's pieces.

So when Reebok did an influencer contest and asked a woman from each continent to design a shoe, Melody took the chance. The fifty shoes she designed went on sale. Over one weekend, instead of selling fifty, she sold 3,000! A few years later, she designed Nike Air Jordans.

At her store, she holds a monthly speaker series. There, the conversations range from story nights to politics. The morning after she hosted Lena Waithe, the first Black woman to win an Emmy Award for writing a comedy series, Melody was the talk of Fairfax Avenue. Having seen the long line outside of her store, folks asked, "What did you drop last night?" To which she responded, "I dropped knowledge!"

فرفان إسمائلى زاده

FARNAZ ESMAEILZADEH

b. 1988

FARNAZ ESMAEILZADEH doesn't climb. She glides and leaps. She has grace, agility, and power. Nicknamed "Spider Woman," Farnaz is a member of the Iranian National Climbing Team. As a speed climber, she has won championships in Iran, Asia, Europe, and North America. She's been a competitive rock-climber since she was thirteen years old, but she started with nothing. No rock-climbing gyms. No coaches. No fellow climbers. No one was rock climbing in Borujerd, where she was born. But that didn't get in her way. She mountaineered with her parents and spent time in nature.

The first wall she climbed was made by her brother in her family's backyard. When she eventually joined a gym, it was only open for limited hours, and there weren't very many qualified climbing coaches. She struggled to get funding to go to competitions. As an Iranian, she had difficulty obtaining visas to travel. But, she says, "I didn't want to be normal. I wanted to climb and follow my dream." And she did.

At the height of her competitive career, in 2013, she was ranked sixth in the world by the International Federation of Sport Climbing. She blazed a trail for other women and girls to pursue climbing. With the help of her mom and four other women, she established the sport of climbing in Zanjan, a northwestern Iranian city where she grew up.

Farnaz now lives in Canada and is assembling her bright future. She's coaching a new generation of climbers. Trailblazing, climbing, and coaching aren't her only talents, though. When she was twenty-one years old, she published her first book, *Pause*.

Her advice to others is: "The circumstances of your life don't make your life. It's your approach to them that makes your life." Thinking like a rock-climber who has to piece together a giant puzzle, she says, "For me, climbing is part of life, a symbol of overcoming the barriers in life."

Farnaz has certainly made her mark!

GOLSHIFTEH FARAHANI
b. 1983

GOLSHIFTEH FARAHANI says, "I surf between different kinds of cinema: blockbusters, big budget, no budget, independent." The multi-talented, internationally recognized actor has starred in big-budget movies like *Pirates of the Caribbean: Dead Men Tell No Tales* with Johnny Depp, *Extraction* with Chris Hemsworth, and *Body of Lies* with Leonardo DiCaprio. She has also worked on independent films like *Paterson* with Adam Driver, and has portrayed strong Spanish, Tunisian, Lebanese, and American characters. She even played a Kurdish combat leader in *Girls of the Sun.*

Born and raised in Iran, Golshifteh grew up in a family of entertainers. Her parents and sister are actors, and her father is also a screenwriter. She was six years old when she started acting. But the love of playing piano had her thinking about a move to Vienna where she could really hone her musical talents. When she was fourteen years old, though, her trajectory changed and acting took a front seat. She won the prize for Best Actress at the Fajr International Film Festival for her first feature film, *The Pear Tree.*

As a teenager in Iran, she would shave her hair and call herself Ameer, a boy's name. With a shaved head, she would become invisible and could play basketball on the streets like the boys.

Not only does Golshifteh know five languages—Farsi, English, French, Arabic, and Kurdish—but she also played in an underground rock band called Kooch Neshin (Nomads). She was a vocalist and played the piano, flute, and harmonica!

In 2012, her life took another turn when the Iranian government didn't like her photograph in a French magazine. Since then, she's been living in France. When asked how living in exile informs her work as an artist, she replied, "You need something in your creative bank to understand different sensations...Exile added to this bank account of... emotions."

NIAZ KASRAVI
b. 1973

NIAZ KASRAVI was nine years old when she and her family moved to the U.S. from Iran. By then, the shadows of the 1979 Revolution had passed, but the blaze of war between her country and its neighbor, Iraq, still scorched the land.

In her homeland, she had experienced feeling different as a Zoroastrian, a religious minority, amongst a mix of Muslims, the religious majority. She had been excused from mandatory weekly Islamic studies at school, but had to submit a document that showed she was studying the Zoroastrian religion. Fast-forward to her California college classroom, when her professor peeled away a new layer of her adopted country. That's when Niaz became aware of inequalities in America. It was a surprise to learn that her new, beloved country was also tainted — that color, class, and creed could shape the trajectory of one's life here too. Niaz yearned to learn and do more.

She studied Criminology, Law and Society. When she joined the National Association for the Advancement of Colored People (NAACP), a civil rights organization, she led campaigns to end racial profiling — the practice of using a person's race or ethnicity to target individuals for a suspicion of a crime — in New York City. She also worked on wrongful sentencing cases, like that of John McNeil in Georgia.

Niaz's most cherished memory was the look of hope two wrongfully convicted men gave one another after she successfully helped lead an initiative to abolish the death penalty in Maryland. In the spring and summer of 2020, she found the cascading social justice movements around the world to be encouraging.

Niaz believes in the best version of America. In the U.S., the right to dissent is invaluable. She seizes this opportunity to help create a more just and equitable country for all of us.

It's no surprise, then, to see her following her own passionate path, despite what others think. "Fitting in is overrated!" she says.

KATAYOUN KHOSROWYAR
b. 1987

KATAYOUN KHOSROWYAR put Iranian women's soccer on the map. When she was sixteen years old, no one could imagine women playing soccer seriously in Iran. But Katayoun was scouted on her first family trip to Iran. She then moved there, helped to assemble a national soccer team, played, coached, and studied chemical engineering in college.

Growing up in Oklahoma, Katayoun started playing soccer when she was five. Her dad, who had moved from Iran as a child, instilled the importance of sportsmanship and athleticism to Katayoun. She was only twenty-six years old when she became the first Iranian woman with a Fédération Internationale de Football Association (FIFA) "A" Coaching License. Two years later, she became the head coach of the Iranian women's soccer team and recruited younger players. Her team won championships. Women playing soccer became the buzz all over Iran!

Alas, the road to athletic stardom was full of push and blocks. In 2011, minutes before Katayoun and her teammates began playing in their second round of Olympic qualifications, a FIFA representative disqualified them for covering their hair. All female athletes representing Iran had to wear a compulsory hijab. But FIFA had been pushing female athletes to wear shorter and tighter uniforms. Eight years of preparation was lost over a head covering!

It took Katayoun years to fight the oppressive FIFA ban. Finally, in 2014, all female athletes who covered their hair for religious reasons were allowed to play. Their inclusion impacted countless female soccer players around the world.

Katayoun believes that soccer is a metaphor for life. "Soccer… teaches the importance of getting back up when you fall, taking care of your mind, body, and soul so you always feel confident."

Katayoun says she wished that when she was younger, she hadn't "taken playing soccer [in the U.S.] for granted." Athletes in Iran have had to fight against barriers, unimaginable to many in the U.S.

MARYAM MIRZAKHANI

1977–2017

MARYAM MIRZAKHANI was the only woman and only Iranian yet to receive the highest prize in mathematics — the Fields Medal.

Until she discovered math, Maryam loved reading and wanted to become a novelist. To her delight, math and literature had many similarities. Equally subject to critical review, both involved endless curiosity and creativity.

Maryam's first math teacher in Tehran thought Maryam didn't have mathematical aptitude, but it was too late — Maryam was already hooked. She approached problem-solving the same way a storyteller unravels a tale. Mathematics allowed her imagination to wander. She doodled, sketched, and found solutions on vast swaths of paper on the floor, just the way a storyteller makes sense of chaos and creates a world out of her imagination.

In 1999, decades before we could imagine a U.S. president instituting a Muslim travel ban, she moved to the U.S. to continue her studies. Her work opened up new vistas in mathematics. Among other things, she created a solution to how many simple loops (curves that don't intersect) are on a given hyperbolic surface, like a potato chip or an industrial plant. Although it's too early to tell how the applications of her work will revolutionize mathematics, it is certain that they will be a springboard for new generations of mathematicians, who are artists in their own right.

For Maryam, limits didn't exist!

SHIRIN NESHAT
b. 1957

SHIRIN NESHAT moved to California from Iran when she was seventeen. At that time, she didn't know that she wouldn't see her family again for at least a dozen years, nor would she return to Iran for almost two decades. The events of history changed her life. In 1979, Iran had a revolution that was followed by a war, barring her return.

She studied art in California, but it was her first visit back to Iran in 1990 that fueled her imagination. She found a country entirely transformed by revolution and war. During Iran's war with Iraq, which lasted most of the 1980s, Iranian women had been called upon to bear arms against the enemy. Shirin was intrigued by the paradox that women who nurture life can also be symbols of war and death. And so, she created a still photography series called *Women of Allah,* which featured images of women donning a chador and holding a gun with Persian calligraphy painted on their hands and face. In her words, "Every image, every woman's submissive gaze, suggests a far more complex and paradoxical reality behind the surface." She received much critical acclaim and her work continues to be studied. Since then, she has worked in still photography, video, and film.

Though she never expected to become a narrator of history, her work is rooted in telling stories from corners around the world. She has worked in Azerbaijan, Egypt, and various parts of the U.S. She says, "The only reason I became an artist was the urgency of my life experiences. The work I make comes out of urgency."

MARJANE SATRAPI
b. 1969

MARJANE SATRAPI let the genie out of the bottle when she wrote her autobiographical graphic novel, *Persepolis*. The novel gave readers a rare behind-the-scenes glimpse of life in Iran. As a child, Marjane was caught in an inevitable revolution and the ensuing war, then moved to Europe as a teenager. Marjane, like the character in her novel, moves in time, place, and language.

Encouraged by her friends and inspired by Art Spiegelman, who wrote the iconic graphic novel *Maus*, Marjane penned her own experiences. And readers loved it! *Persepolis* went on to win many awards, and now—decades after its publication—students from middle school to college still read it!

The book was temporarily even banned in Chicago and Lebanon. Some speculated that it was because of its portrayal of Iran's Islamic regime and could possibly be offensive to Muslim students. Others noted that its depiction of violence might be inappropriate for seventh-grade students.

Marjane was born in Rasht, a northern Iranian city on the Caspian Sea. She moved to Austria, when she was fourteen, and eventually to her adopted country of France. When she didn't think she would make it as an artist, she considered becoming a private detective.

Marjane is an accomplished author, illustrator, painter, and filmmaker. In 2020, she released, *Radioactive,* a film about Marie Curie. Marjane wove threads of war, chaos, and obstacles in that story, just as she did in *Persepolis*. The heroines in the film follow one of her maxims: "Take your rights because no one will give them to you."

Marjane's sense of humor is infectious. In conversation, she smiles and laughs. In preparation for an interview at the New York Public Library, she was asked to write a seven-word autobiography in a form of a haiku (a traditionally Japanese poem that has three lines and seventeen syllables). She wrote, "I do not like seven. Seven sucks."

EPILOGUE

Kahlil Gibran, the Lebanese-American writer and poet, wrote, "We are limited, not by our abilities, but by our vision." Was he talking about his eyesight when he penned this quote? No. He was referring to the courage we must have to live the life we imagine for ourselves.

The heroines in this book faced hurdles not unlike those you, or someone you know, have experienced. They felt unwelcomed. They questioned their own judgment. They felt ugly. They thought they were out of place. They did things that no one had ever imagined doing. Doors slammed in their faces. They had upsets and setbacks. They were stonewalled and gaslighted.

So, how did they become trailblazers? Did where they hail from make a difference? Maybe. They — or their parents — were born and raised in a different place from some of you. Was it easy? Absolutely not! They all had a vision of who they wanted to become. They had energy that waxed and waned. They did difficult things — sometimes not well. They made practical and impractical decisions. They were deliberate, and from time to time unlucky. They were confident, but not always. They were wounded and recovered. They were persistent. They found allies. They were brave.

Their path was messy. And that's the point. No matter where you come from, becoming the best version of yourself will not be easy.

As you put this book aside, I hope that you have gleaned a window into other women's experiences and found your reflection in them too. Ask, *What will hold me back*? Will you let the limited imagination of naysayers paint your future? Your opinion of yourself is the most important one in the room.

Be courageous and take a chance. Stay focused on what it takes to be the best version of you. Tackle tough goals. Charge the field!

Rumi, the Iranian poet, said, "Set your sights on a place higher than your eyes can see." Remember these women with mettle, and all they achieved.

CHAPTER NOTES

CHAPTER 1: ANOUSHEH ANSARI

Ansari, Anousheh. Interviewed by Yasmine Mahdavi on March 6, 2018.

Ansari, Anousheh. *My Dream of Stars*. New York: St. Martin's Griffin, 2010.

Ansari, Anousheh. "Price of a Dream," Space Blog, September 14, 2006, http://spaceblog.xprize.org/2006/09/14/price-of-a-dream.

Brookings. "Order from Chaos: The Iranian Revolution — A Timeline of Events," retrieved May 23, 2019, https://www.brookings.edu/blog/order-from-chaos/2019/01/24/the-iranian-revolution-a-timeline-of-events.

"Climates to Travel: World Climate Guide," retrieved May 23, 2019, https://www.climatestotravel.com/climate/iran#mountains.

Dash, Eric, et al. "America's 40 Richest Under 40," *Fortune*, September 17, 2001, https://archive.fortune.com/magazines/fortune/fortune_archive/2001/09/17/310275/index.htm.

Encyclopedia Britannica. "Anousheh Ansari: American Businesswoman," retrieved on March 19, 2019, https://www.britannica.com/biography/Anousheh-Ansari.

Fakhredin Blog. "Anousheh Ansari, the first Persian astronaut." August 26, 2006, http://fakhredinblog-en.blogspot.com/2006/08/anousheh-ansari-persian-astronaut.html?m=1.

Hakimzadeh, Shirin. "Iran: A Vast Diaspora Abroad and Millions of Refugees at Home," Migration Policy Institute, September 1, 2006, https://www.migrationpolicy.org/article/iran-vast-diaspora-abroad-and-millions-refugees-home.

Hogendijk, Jan P. "Sharaf al-Dīn al-ūsī on the number of positive roots of cubic equations." *Historia Mathematica*, Vol. 16, Iss. 1, February 1989, p. 69–85.

Office of the Historian: A Short History of the Department of State. "The Iranian Hostage Crisis," Retrieved on June 19, 2019, https://history.state.gov/departmenthistory/short-history/iraniancrises.

O'Callaghan, Jonathon. "Twenty-One Inspirational and Historic Space Quotes You Need to Know," June 25, 2013, https://www.spaceanswers.com/space-exploration/can-astronauts-phone-home-whenever-they-want.

Names withheld. "Life Under the Shah," December 6, 1979, https://www.thecrimson.com/article/1979/12/6/life-under-the-shah-pit-was.

Richardson Economic Development Partnership. "Home to the Telecom Corridor." Retrieved September 1, 2020, https://www.telecomcorridor.com.

TTARA Research Foundation. "The Telecommunications Industry in the Texas Economy and Tax System," April 2005, https://www.ttara.org/wp-content/uploads/2018/09/TelecommunicationsIndustryTexas_5-05.pdf.

Voices and Visions. "Jimmy Carter Toasts the Shah | 31 December 1971," retrieved May 23, 2019, http://vandvreader.org/jimmy-carter-toasts-the-shah-31-december-1977.

CHAPTER 1 SIDEBARS

Encyclopaedia Britannica, s.v. "Iraq under Saddam Hussein," retrieved February 14, 2018, https://www.britannica.com/biography/Ayatollah-Muhammad-Baqir-al-Sadr.

Encyclopaedia Britannica, s.v. "Khūzestān," retrieved February 14, 2018, https://www.britannica.com/place/Khuzestan.

Gallagher, Mike. "The 'Beauty' and the Horror of the Iran–Iraq War," BBC News, September 26, 2015, http://www.bbc.com/news/magazine-34353349.

"The Iran-Contra Affair," United States History, retrieved February 14, 2018, http://www.u-s-history.com/pages/h1889.html.

The History Channel. "Iran–Iraq War," *History Channel* article, retrieved February 14, 2018, http://www.history.com/topics/iran-iraq-war.

CHAPTER 2: MINA BISSELL

Academy of Achievement. "Ruth Bader Ginsburg," Achievement.org, retrieved October 19, 2020, https://achievement.org/achiever/ruth-bader-ginsburg.

Azvolinsky, Anna. "Location, Location, Location," *The Scientist*, April 1, 2017, http://www.the-scientist.com/?articles.view/articleNo/48909/title/Location--Location--Location.

Bissell, Mina. Interviewed by Yasmine Mahdavi on February 13, 2018.

Bissell, Mina. "Heeding a mentor's advice: A lesson in persistence," *Nature Cell Biology*, 2011, 13, 1386, http://www.nature.com/articles/ncb2392.

Bissell, Mina. "Thinking in three dimensions: Discovering reciprocal signaling between the extracellular matrix and nucleus and the wisdom of microenvironment and tissue architecture," *Molecular Biology of the Cell*, November 1, 2016, 27(21): 3205–3209, https://www.ncbi.nlm.nih.gov/pmc/articles/PMC5170853.

Geiler, Kelly. "*Protein Folding: The Good, The Bad, and The Ugly,*" Harvard University, Graduate School of Arts and Sciences, retrieved May 24, 2019, http://sitn.hms.harvard.edu/flash/2010/issue65.

Ginsburg, Justice Ruth Bader. "The Changing Complexion of Harvard Law School," *Harvard Women's Law Journal*, Spring 2004, Vol. 27, p. 303, https://heinonline.org/HOL/LandingPage?handle=hein.journals/hwlj27&div=11&id=&page=.

"Iran During World War II," United States Holocaust Memorial Museum, retrieved March 5, 2018, https://www.ushmm.org/wlc/en/article.php?ModuleId=10008209.

Iravani, Mohammad Reza (2011). "Women's Education, Employment and Unemployment in Iran," *Journal of Basic and Applied Scientific Research*, 1 (12): 2965–2970.

Khan Academy. "The extracellular matrix and cell wall," retrieved May 21, 2019, https://www.khanacademy.org/science/biology/structure-of-a-cell/cytoskeleton-junctions-and-extracellular-structures/a/the-extracellular-matrix-and-cell-wall.

Kolata, Gina. "In War on Cancer, Old Ideas Can Lead to Fresh Directions," *The New York Times,* December 29, 2009, http://www2.lbl.gov/LBL-Programs/lifesciences/BissellLab/articles/2009New%20York%20Times%20Article.pdf.

Minding the Workplace. "What is academic tenure?" The New Workplace Institute Blog, December 2017, https://newworkplace.wordpress.com/2011/08/22/what-is-academic-tenure.

People Behind the Science Podcast. "327: Dr. Mina Bissell: Changing How We Think About Cancer by Revealing the Critical Role of Context in Tissue Specificity," PBS, January 11, 2016, http://www.peoplebehindthescience.com/dr-mina-bissell.

Reilein, Amy. Associate Research Scientist at Columbia University. Email correspondence with Yasmine Mahdavi, May 24, 2019 and September 14, 2020.

Short, Ben. "Mina Bissell: Context is everything," *Journal of Cell Biology,* 2009, 185(3): 374, http://jcb.rupress.org/content/185/3/374.short.

Science Museum. "What are proteins made of?" The National Archives, retrieved May 24, 2019, https://webarchive.nationalarchives.gov.uk/20160802150903/http://www.sciencemuseum.org.uk/whoami/findoutmore/yourbody/whatdoyourcellsdo/whatisacellmadeof/whatareproteinsmadeof

Zagorski, Nick. "Mina J. Bissell: Going the Extra Mile … and Dimension," *ASBMB Today,* October 2010, http://www2.lbl.gov/LBLPrograms/lifesciences/BissellLab/articles/ASBMB_Today_Oct_2010_Mina_Feature.pdf.

CHAPTER 2 SIDEBARS

AAUW. "Even in High-Paying STEM Fields, Women Are Shortchanged," American Association of University Women, April 14, 2015, https://www.aauw.org/2015/04/14/women-shortchanged-in-stem.

Arfa, Hassan. "Reza Shah Pahlavi," *Encyclopedia Britannica,* retrieved January 20, 2018, https://www.britannica.com/biography/Reza-Shah-Pahlavi.

Association for Women in Science. "Advocacy," AWIS Action Network, retrieved February 13, 2018, https://www.awis.org/advocacy.

European Commission. "Challenging Futures of Science in Society: Emerging Trends and Cutting-Edge Issues," The Masis Report, 2009, http://ec.europa.eu/research/science-society/document_library/pdf_06/the-masis-report_en.pdf, p. 44.

Henriksen, Ellen Karoline, Justin Dillon, and Jim Ryder, eds. *Understanding Student Participation and Choice in Science and Technology Education.* London: Springer, 2015, p. 49.

Latimer, John Francis. *What's Happened to Our High Schools?* Whitefish, MT: Literary Licensing, 2012.

My College Options and STEMConnector. "Where Are the STEM Students?" *The Daily Herald,* 2013, https://www.dailyherald.com/assets/PDF/DA127758822.pdf.

National Girls Collaborative Project. "Statistics," National Girls Collaborative Project, retrieved February 13, 2018, https://ngcproject.org/statistics.

National Girls Collaborative Project. "The State of Women and Girls in STEM," National Girls Collaborative Project, August 2016, https://ngcproject.org/sites/default/files/ngcp_the_state_of_girls_and_women_in_stem_2016_final.pdf.

National Science Board. "Science & Engineering Indicators: 2016," National Science Foundation, last updated August 3, 2016, https://nsf.gov/statistics/2016/nsb20161/uploads/1/nsb20161.pdf.

NOVA's Secret Life of Scientists and Engineers. "Mayim Bialik: Blossoming to Science," YouTube video, 4 min 14 sec, February 14, 2013, https://www.youtube.com/watch?time_continue=234&v=TZt-JTdfXjw.

Popova, Maria. "How to Save Science: Education, the Gender Gap, and the Next Generation of Creative Thinkers," BrainPickings, retrieved February 13, 2018, https://www.brainpickings.org/index.php/2013/02/12/saving-our-science-anissa-ramirez.

Ramirez, Ainissa. *Save Our Science: How to Inspire a New Generation of Scientists,* TED Conferences, 2013.

Ruby, Jessica. "Ainissa Ramirez on women in STEM," TED-Ed blog, September 18, 2013, http://blog.ed.ted.com/2013/09/18/ainissa-ramirez-on-women-in-stem.

Shen, Helen. "Inequality quantified: Mind the gender gap," *Nature,* March 6, 2013, http://www.nature.com/news/inequality-quantified-mind-the-gender-gap-1.12550#/hurdles.

Tripathi, Deepak. *Imperial Designs: War, Humiliation & the Making of History,* Washington, D.C.: Potomac Books, 2013.

Women You Should Know. "13-Year-Old Aspiring Astronaut's Inspirational Speech at the March for Science," WYSK, April 24, 2017, http://womenyoushouldknow.net/13-year-old-aspiring-astronauts-inspirational-speech-at-the-march-for-science.

Women You Should Know. "Mayim Bialik Encouraging Girls to Pursue Careers in STEM," WYSK, February 25, 2014, http://womenyoushouldknow.net/mayim-bialik-encouraging-girls-pursue-careers-stem.

CHAPTER 3: DORSA DERAKHSHANI

Chasmar, Jessica. "Iranian Chess Master Booted from National Team for Not Wearing Islamic Head Covering," *The Washington Times,* February 25, 2017, https://www.washingtontimes.com/news/2017/feb/25/dorsa-derakhshani-iranian-chess-master-booted-from.

"Chess Openings," The Chess Website, retrieved on May 20, 2019, http://www.thechesswebsite.com/chess-openings.

Dehghan, Saeed Kamali. "Boycott of women's chess championship would 'hurt women in Iran,'" *The Guardian,* September 30, 2016, https://www.theguardian.com/world/2016/sep/30/boycott-of-womens-world-chess-championship-iran-tehran.

Derakhshani, Dorsa (@dorsa.derakhshani). 2020. "I'm published for something other than chess biology is niceeeee," Instagram photo, February 4, 2020, https://www.instagram.com/p/B8KGoi8nnfe.

Derakhshani, Dorsa. Instagram direct message exchange with Yasmine Mahdavi on October 6, 2020.

Derakhshani, Dorsa. "On Chess: How Chess Can Prepare You for Medical School," St. Louis Public Radio, March 5, 2020, https://news.stlpublicradio.org/post/chess-how-chess-can-prepare-you-medical-school.

Derakhshani, Dorsa. "Take Your Freedom of Choice Seriously," TEDx Talks, YouTube, 13 min 39 sec, August 22, 2019, https://www.youtube.com/watch?v=dnPmfzAGkcU.

Derakhshani, Dorsa. "Why I Left Iran to Play Chess in America," *The New York Times*, December 29, 2017, https://www.nytimes.com/2017/12/29/opinion/iran-chess-woman-america.html.

"Dorsa Derakhshani vs. Mark Plotkin," Chessgames.com, retrieved September 1, 2020, https://www.chessgames.com/perl/chessgame?gid=1872556.

Fernandez, John. "What Does It Feel Like to Play a Chess Grandmaster?" *HuffPost*, October 12, 2016, updated October 13, 2017, https://www.huffpost.com/entry/what-does-it-feel-like-to_b_12456934.

Hauser, Christine, and Maya Salam. "Iranian Chess Player, Shunned for Refusing to Wear Hijab, Will Play in U.S.," *The New York Times*, October 3, 2017, https://www.nytimes.com/2017/10/03/world/middleeast/chess-hijab-iran.html.

Klein, Mike. "Chess and the Hijab: Iran's Dorsa Derakhshani Finds Her Way," Wbur.org, Boston's NPR News Station, September 29, 2017, http://www.wbur.org/onlyagame/2017/09/29/chess-hijab-dorsa-derakhshani.

Klein, Mike. "Ousted Iranian Player: 'My Wardrobe Should Not Be Anyone's Business," Chess.com, updated March 1, 2017, https://www.chess.com/news/view/ousted-iranian-player-my-wardrobe-should-not-be-anyone-s-business-4013.

Lammers, Markus. "Interview with Dorsa Derakhshani," Beyond Chess, December 23, 2016, http://beyond-chess.com/interview-dorsa-Derakhshani.

Payne, Marissa. "Teenage Iranian Chess Master Banned from National Team for Refusing to Wear a Headscarf," *The Washington Post*, February 21, 2017, https://www.washingtonpost.com/news/early-lead/wp/2017/02/21/teenage-iranian-chess-master-banned-from-national-team-for-refusing-to-wear-a-headscarf/?utm_term=.ede909db7f3b.

Peterson, Macauley. "Dorsa Derakhshani: From Iran to the USA (Part 2)," Chess News, March 29, 2020, https://en.chessbase.com/post/dorsa-derakhshani-2.

Rogers, Katie. "American Chess Player Boycotts Championship in Iran Over Hijab Rule," *The New York Times*, October 7, 2016, https://www.nytimes.com/2016/10/08/sports/american-chess-player-boycotts-championship-that-would-require-her-to-wear-a-hijab.html?smid=fb-nytimes&smtyp=cur.

Saint Louis Chess Club. "2019 Pan-Ams vs. Brendan Zhang | Chess and Psychology," YouTube, 53 min 53 sec, https://www.youtube.com/watch?v=6dMtuxZ2uQk.

A note on chess ratings: In order to earn the WIM title, a female player needs a minimum rating of 1850 and has to play against other females of equivalent capabilities. The IM minimum rating is 2050, 200 points higher than the WIM rating. The minimum rating for the WGM title (which is only open to females who qualify) is 2000. In contrast, the GM title is 2200, again, 200 points higher than the equivalent women's rating.

CHAPTER 3 SIDEBARS

"A Brief History of the Veil in Islam," Facing History and Ourselves, retrieved January 24, 2018, https://www.facinghistory.org/civic-dilemmas/brief-history-veil-islam.

Abu-Lughod, Lila. *Do Muslim Women Need Saving?* New York: Harvard University Press, 2013.

Ahmadov, Zahir. "Women in Chess—A Matter of Opinion," *Chess News*, September 21, 2007, https://en.chessbase.com/post/women-in-che-a-matter-of-opinion.

Aman, Fatemah. "Iran's Headscarf Politics," Middle East Institute, November 3, 2014, http://www.mei.edu/content/article/irans-headscarf-politics.

"Cross-Cultural Head Coverings," Center for South Asian & Middle Eastern Studies, University of Illinois at Urbana-Champaign, retrieved January 28, 2018, http://www.csames.illinois.edu/documents/outreach/Cross-Culture_Head_Coverings.pdf.

Dearden, Lizzie. "Iranian Women Call on Western Tourists to Violate Hijab Law to Fight Against Oppression," *The Independent*, April 22, 2016, http://www.independent.co.uk/news/world/middle-east/iranian-women-in-my-stealthy-freedom-campaign-call-on-western-tourists-to-violate-headscarf-law-to-a6996136.html.

FIDE. "Chess Ratings: Advanced Search Results," International Chess Federation, retrieved September 21, 2020, http://ratings.fide.com/advaction.phtml?idcode=&name=&title=g&other_title=&country=%25&sex=&srating=0&erating=3000&birthday=&radio=name&line=asc.

Freund, Richard. "The Veiling of Women in Judaism, Christianity and Islam: A Guide to the Exhibition," Maurice Greenberg Center for Judaic Studies, 2012, http://uhaweb.hartford.edu/greenberg-center/Veiled%20Women%20Catalog.pdf.

Lockett, Jon. "Fears for Hijab-Waving 'Hero,'" *The Sun*, January 23, 2018, https://www.thesun.co.uk/news/5404426/brave-iranian-woman-who-stood-on-tehran-pillar-box-waving-her-hijab-in-protest-vanishes-and-is-feared-arrested-lawyer-says.

Merim Bilalić, Kieran Smallbone, Peter McLeod, and Fernand Gobet. "Why Are (the Best) Women So Good at Chess? Participation Rates and Gender Differences in Intellectual Domains," *Proc. R. Soc. B* (2009) 276, p. 1161–1165, http://rspb.royalsocietypublishing.org/content/276/1659/1161.

Moaveni, Azadeh. "Your Boycott Won't Help Iranian Women," *The New York Times*, October 7, 2016, https://www.nytimes.com/2016/10/08/opinion/your-boycott-wont-help-iranian-women.html.

Raphael, Sarah. "Women Are Pushed to Be Just Bodies—Veiled Under Religion or Veiled by Makeup," Refinery29, June 7, 2018, https://www.refinery29.com/en-gb/2018/06/200895/nawal-el-saadawi-interview.

Safai, Darya. "Western Feminists Snub an Iranian Heroine," *The Wall Street Journal*, March 1, 2017, https://www.wsj.com/articles/western-feminists-snub-an-iranian-heroine-1488413022.

World Chess Federation. "Chess Ratings," World Chess Federation website, retrieved January 19, 2018, http://ratings.fide.com/advaction.phtml?idcode=&name=&title=g&other_title=&country=&sex=&srating=0&erating=3000&birthday=&radio=&ex_

rated=&line=asc&inactiv=&offset=100; http://ratings.fide.com/
advaction.phtml?idcode=&name=&title=g&other_title=&country=%&sex
=f&srating=0&erating=3000&birthday=&radio=country&line=asc.

Yong, Ed. "Why Are There So Few Female Grandmasters?"
ScienceBlogs, December 23, 2008, http://scienceblogs.com/
notrocketscience/2008/12/23/why-are-there-so-few-female-chess-
grandmasters.

CHAPTER 4: ANNA ESKAMANI

Chingos, Matthew M. "The Impact of a Universal Class-Size Reduction Policy:
Evidence from Florida's Statewide Mandate," Harvard University, Program
on Education Policy and Governance, May 2010, p. 3,
https://fordhaminstitute.org/national/commentary/impact-universal-
class-size-reduction-policy-evidence-floridas-statewide.

Eskamani, Anna. "Did You Catch Anna on Vice News?" Anna for
Florida website, November 1, 2018, https://www.annaforflorida.
com/2018/11/01/did-you-catch-anna-on-vice-news.

Eskamani, Anna. "My Mother's Name Is Nasrin," YouTube video, 2 min 11 sec,
September 12, 2018, https://www.youtube.com/watch?v=AVket6Bp4p0v.

Eskamani, Anna. "The Story Behind the Logo," YouTube video, 2 min 12 sec,
June 6, 2018, https://www.youtube.com/watch?v=s2EmaP7O_gc.

Eskamani, Anna. "Yes, I Am a Woman Running for Office and Yes, I Curse,"
Florida Politics blog post, September 28, 2018, http://floridapolitics.com/
archives/276027-anna-eskamani-yes-i-am-a-woman-running-for-office-
and-yes-i-curse.

Eskamani, Anna. Interviewed by Yasmine Mahdavi on December 13, 2018.

Eskamani, Ida. "Why I'm #TeamAnna," Anna for Florida website, August 26,
2018, https://www.annaforflorida.com/2018/08/26/why-im-teamanna-
ida-eskamani.

Gillespie, Ryan. "Anna Eskamani Surpasses $500K in Area's Most Expensive
State House Race," Orlando Sentinel, October 24, 2018, https://www.
orlandosentinel.com/news/politics/political-pulse/os-ne-anna-eskamani-
fundraising-milestone-20181024-story.html.

Gillespie, Ryan. "Florida House Race between Anna Eskamani, Stockton
Reeves One of Area's Most Contested," Orlando Sentinel, October 2, 2018,
https://www.orlandosentinel.com/news/politics/political-pulse/os-ne-
house-district-47-ads-20181002-story.html.

Gillespie, Ryan. "Former President Barack Obama Endorses Democrats
Andrew Gillum, Stephanie Murphy, Nancy Soderberg, Anna Eskamani,"
Orlando Sentinel, October 1, 2018, https://www.orlandosentinel.
com/news/politics/political-pulse/os-ne-obama-endorses-florida-
democrats20181001-story.html.

Magane, Azmia. "Five Questions for Anna Eskamani, the First Iranian-
American Elected to the Florida Legislature," Teen Vogue, November 8,
2018, https://www.teenvogue.com/story/anna-eskamani-first-iranian-
american-elected-to-florida-legislature.

Pellisier, Hank. "Inside the 5th Grader's Brain: What Insights Can Neuroscience
Offer Parents about the Mind of a Fifth Grader?" GreatSchools.org, July
16, 2016, https://www.greatschools.org/gk/articles/fifth-grader-brain-
development.

Powers, Scott. "Eskamani Gains Backing of Iranian-American Group," *Florida Politics*, May 30, 2018, http://floridapolitics.com/archives/264921-anna-eskamani-gains-backing-of-national-iranian-american-group.

Powers, Scott. "Stockton Reeves' New TV Ad Paints Anna Eskamani as Radical," *Florida Politics*, October 19, 2018, http://floridapolitics.com/archives/278248-stockton-reeves-new-tv-ad-paints-anna-eskamani-as-radical.

The Public Affairs Alliance of Iranian Americans. "Iranian American Women Make History," PAAIA website, November 7, 2018, https://paaia.org/CMS/iranian-american-women-make-history.aspx.

Roose, Kevin, and Sheera Frenkel. "4,500 Tech Workers, 1 Mission: Get Democrats Elected," *The New York Times*, July 13, 2018, https://www.nytimes.com/2018/07/13/technology/tech-midterms-democrats.html.

School Board of Orange County. "Code of Conduct," retrieved May 16, 2019, https://www.ocps.net/UserFiles/Servers/Server_54619/File/Frequently%20Updated%20Documents/Code%20of%20Conduct.pdf.

WKMG News 6 ClickOrlando. "Florida House Candidate Anna Eskamani Discusses Health Care on *The Weekly*," YouTube Video, 18 min 41 sec, October 7, 2018, https://www.youtube.com/watch?v=fOQBZ2XBQvg.

CHAPTER 4 SIDEBARS

ABC News. "Malala Yousafzai, 16, and Her Miraculous Story of Surviving Being Shot by the Taliban," YouTube, 4 min 40 sec, October 11, 2013, https://www.youtube.com/watch?v=CXvs1vwiD0M.

Alabed, Bana. *Dear World: A Syrian Girl's Story of War and Plea for Peace*, New York: Simon & Schuster, 2017.

Alabed, Bana. "You don't have to wait to be an adult to be a leader," August 10, 2020, 12:24pm, https://twitter.com/AlabedBana/status/1292874422622269441.

"Anna Kaplan for New York State Senate," Anna for NY Senate, retrieved February 1, 2019, https://annafornysenate.com.

Astor, Maggie. "Seven Times in History When Students Turned to Activism," *The New York Times,* March 5, 2018, https://www.nytimes.com/2018/03/05/us/student-protest-movements.html.

Cumming, Ed. "Xiuhtezcatl Roske-Martinez: 'Our greed is destroying the planet,'" *The Guardian*, October 9, 2015, https://www.theguardian.com/environment/2015/oct/09/xiuhtezcatl-roske-martinez-earth-guardians.

Durkin, Erin. "'It's About Time': Shirley Chisholm, First Black Congresswoman, Will Get a Statue," *The Guardian*, December 5, 2018, https://www.google.com/amp/s/amp.theguardian.com/us-news/2018/dec/05/its-about-time-shirley-chisholm-first-black-congresswoman-will-get-a-statue.

Dyer, Candice. "A Handshake Lawyer from Lafayette: Zahra Karinshak Speaks Arabic with a Strong Southern Accent," 2017 Georgia Super Lawyers, March 2017, https://www.superlawyers.com/georgia/article/a-handshake-lawyer-from-lafayette/14efcd6b-33e0-49da-b3fe-91e320d0b174.html.

Gorgin, Ira. "Looking Back at Tehran's 1999 Student Protests," RadioFreeEurope, July 9, 2008, https://www.rferl.org/a/Iran_Student_Protests/1182717.html.

Great Neck Record staff. "Anna Kaplan to Run for Congress," *Great Neck Record*, January 13, 2016, https://greatneckrecord.com/anna-kaplan-to-run-for-congress.

"IAPAC Proudly Endorses the Campaign of Zahra Karinshak for Georgia State Senate," PAAIA, May 4, 2018, retrieved February 1, 2019, https://paaia.org/CMS/iapac-proudly-endorses-campaign-zahra-karinshak-georgia-state-senate.aspx.

Kaddoura, Tala. "A 'System of Control': Child Detention in the Occupied West Bank," Al Jazeera, February 27, 2018, https://www.aljazeera.com/news/2018/02/system-control-child-detention-occupied-west-bank-180227071826444.html.

Kestenbaum, Sam. "Meet the Iranian Jew Who's Running for Congress––Despite the Donald Trump Trolls," *Forward*, June 27, 2016, https://forward.com/news/343714/meet-the-iranian-jew-whos-running-for-congress-despite-the-donald-trump-tro.

Levy-Haim, Miriam. "A Persian-Jewish Refugee Who Fled Iran by Airlift Just Became a State Senator in New York," *Tablet*, November 29, 2019, https://www.tabletmag.com/scroll/275782/a-persian-jewish-refugee-who-fled-iran-by-airlift-just-became-a-state-senator-in-new-york.

"Meet the Candidate," Zahra Karinshak for Senate, retrieved February 1, 2019, https://www.votezahra.com/meet-zahra.

"Minors Among 19 Palestinians Detained by Israeli Forces," Ma'an News Agency, December 3, 2018, https://www.maannews.com/Content.aspx?id=781970.

Pimentel, Julia, and Carolyn Bernecca. "20 Young Activists Who Are Changing the World," Complex, December 22, 2018, https://www.complex.com/life/young-activists-who-are-changing-the-world/malala-yousafzai.

Sherwood, Harriet. "The Palestinian Children — Alone and Bewildered — in Israel's Al Jalame Jail," *The Guardian*, January 22, 2012, https://www.theguardian.com/world/2012/jan/22/palestinian-children-detained-jail-israel.

"Statistics on Palestinian Minors in the Custody of Israeli Security Forces," B'Tselem, The Israeli Information Center for Human Rights in the Occupied Territory, last updated January 21, 2019, https://www.btselem.org/statistics/minors_in_custody.

Tamimi, Ahed. Interviewed by Oliver Holmes and Sufian Taha. "Ahed Tamimi: 'I am a freedom fighter. I will not be the victim,'" *The Guardian*, July 30, 2018, https://www.theguardian.com/world/2018/jul/30/ahed-tamimi-i-am-a-freedom-fighter-i-will-not-be-the-victim-palestinian-israel.

Tamimi, Ahed. "Occupied Childhood: Ahed Tamimi Pens a Heartfelt Letter About Life in and After Prison," *Vogue*, October 4, 2018, https://en.vogue.me/fashion/perspectives/ahed-tamimi-palestine-open-letter.

Tamimi, Bissell. Interviewed by the International Solidarity Movement. "Why Ahed slapped the soldier," June 17, 2018, https://palsolidarity.org/2018/06/why-ahed-slapped-the-soldier-an-interview-with-bassem-tamimi.

The New York Times. "A Schoolgirl's Odyssey: Malala Yousafzai Story," YouTube, 19 min 56 sec, October 13, 2009, https://www.youtube.com/watch?v=a6T5DeZ9Z4c.

UNICEF. "Children in Israeli Military Detention: Observations and Recommendations," UNICEF, February 2013, retrieved February 1, 2019, https://www.unicef.org/oPt/UNICEF_oPt_Children_in_Israeli_Military_ Detention_Observations_and_Recommendations_-_6_March_2013.pdf.

Warren, Scott. *Generation Citizen: The Power of Youth in Our Politics.* Berkeley: Counterpoint, 2019.

Yousafzai, Malala. "Nobel lecture, 2014 Peace Prize," December 10, 2014, https://www.nobelprize.org/prizes/peace/2014/yousafzai/26074-malala-yousafzai-nobel-lecture-2014.

Yurcaba, Jo. "A 15-Year-Old Spoke to the UN About Climate Change," *Bustle,* July 5, 2015, https://www.bustle.com/articles/95003-xiuhtezcatl-roske-martinez-a-15-year-old-climate-change-activist-gave-an-incredible-speech-to-the-un.

"Xiuhtezcatl Martinez," Earth Guardians website, retrieved February 1, 2019, https://www.earthguardians.org/xiuhtezcatl.

CHAPTER 5: JASMIN MOGHBELI

Bosch, Bridget. "Maj. Jasmin Moghbeli Astronaut Candidate Interview B-Roll, Camera 1," YouTube video, 6 min 55 sec, June 15, 2017, https://www.youtube.com/watch?v=Y4iui41s59Y.

Clark, Stephen. "NASA unveils a new class of 12 astronauts—Spaceflight Now," *Same Day Newspaper,* June 8, 2017, http://samedaynewspaper.com/nasa-unveils-new-class-of-12-astronauts-spaceflight-now.

Eckstein, Megan. "Marine Maj. Jasmin Moghbeli Selected as NASA Astronaut Candidate, Fulfilling Childhood Dream," USNI News, June 20, 2017, https://news.usni.org/2017/06/20/marine-maj-jasmin-moghbeli-selected-nasa-astronaut-candidate-fulfilling-childhood-dream.

Fecht, Sarah. "How Will We Eat on Mars?" *Popular Science,* January 11, 2016, https://www.popsci.com/how-will-we-eat-on-mars#page-2.

Federov, Gleb. "Why Do Foreign Astronauts Have to Be Able to Speak Russian?" *Russian Beyond,* April 12, 2015, https://www.rbth.com/society/2015/04/12/why_do_foreign_astronauts_have_to_be_able_to_speak_russian_45145.html.

Long, Patrick. "Becoming a NASA Astronaut and Military Service." *The Balance,* updated September 21, 2016, https://www.thebalance.com/so-you-want-to-become-an-astronaut-3345123.

NASA, "Astronaut Candidate Program," Wayback Machine, Internet Archive, retrieved September 1, 2020, https://web.archive.org/web/20100827022721/http://nasajobs.nasa.gov/astronauts/content/AstroCandbro_sm_new.pdf.

NASA. "Astronauts Take a Dive," *NASAexplores,* May 20, 2004, https://www.nasa.gov/audience/foreducators/9-12/features/F_Astronauts_Take_Dive.html.

NASA People. "Astronaut Candidate Program," NASA.gov, retrieved May 17, 2019, https://astronauts.nasa.gov/content/broch00.htm.

NASA People. "Frequently Asked Questions," NASA.gov, retrieved February 7, 2017, https://astronauts.nasa.gov/content/faq.htm.

NASA People. "NASA's Newest Astronaut Recruits to Conduct Research Off the Earth, For the Earth and Deep Space Missions," NASA press release,

June 7, 2017, https://www.nasa.gov/press-release/nasa-s-newest-astronaut-recruits-to-conduct-research-off-the-earth-for-the-earth-and.

"'Not Stopped Smiling Since': NASA's New Astronauts on Being Selected," Madman blog, June 10, 2017, https://space.mindofamadman.com/2017/06/10/not-stopped-smiling-since-nasas-new-astronauts-on-being-selected.

Schogol, Jeff. "Marine Cobra Pilot Aims for New Stars as an Astronaut Candidate," *Marine Corps Times*, June 15, 2017, https://www.marinecorpstimes.com/news/your-marine-corps/2017/06/16/marine-cobra-pilot-aims-for-new-stars-as-an-astronaut-candidate.

Space Camp. "Advanced Space Academy," U.S. Space and Rocket Center, retrieved February 13, 2018, https://www.spacecamp.com/space/advancedacademy.

Wright, Robin. "Jasmin Moghbeli, Badass Astronaut," *The New Yorker*, July 2, 2017, https://www.newyorker.com/news/news-desk/jasmin-moghbeli-americas-badass-immigrant-astronaut.

CHAPTER 5 SIDEBARS

"50 years, 50 giant leaps: How NASA rocked our world," *The Independent*, July 28, 2008, http://www.independent.co.uk/news/science/50-years-50-giant-leaps-how-nasa-rocked-our-world-879377.html.

BBC News. "Great Views. Sleeps Six," BBC, retrieved February 14, 2018, http://www.bbc.co.uk/news/resources/idt-c1dffc35-fe53-492d-a4bf-752a22bd1ebc.

"Ceradyne," 3M website, retrieved February 1, 2018, https://www.3m.com/3M/en_US/design-and-specialty-materials-us/ceradyne.

"Charshanbeh Soori," Historical Iranian Sites and People, March 11, 2010, http://historicaliran.blogspot.com/2010/03/charshanbeh-soori.html.

Chow, Denise. "Everyday Tech From Space: How Moon Science Gave Us the DustBuster," SPACE.com, January 14, 2011, https://www.space.com/10625-space-spinoff-technology-handheld-vacuum.html.

Cool Cosmos. "How Fast Does the Space Station Travel?" NASA, retrieved February 14, 2018, http://coolcosmos.ipac.caltech.edu/ask/282-How-fast-does-the-Space-Station-travel-.

"Digital vs. Conventional Radiography in the Dental Office," The Canadian Academy of Dental Health and Community Sciences, August 26, 2014, https://www.canadianacademyofdentalhygiene.ca/blog/digital-vs-conventional-radiography-dental-office.html.

Documentary Tube. "An Inside Tour of the International Space Station," YouTube video, 28 min 57 sec, December 24, 2014, https://www.youtube.com/watch?v=bhGydridbEA.

European Space Agency. "Building the International Space Station," December 11, 2002, http://www.esa.int/Our_Activities/Human_Spaceflight/International_Space_Station/Building_the_International_Space_Station.

European Space Agency. "Where Is the International Space Station?" Retrieved February 14, 2018, http://www.esa.int/Our_Activities/Human_Spaceflight/International_Space_Station/Where_is_the_International_Space_Station.

"FINDER Search and Rescue Technology Helped Save Lives in Nepal," Jet Propulsion Laboratory, California Institute of Technology, May 7, 2015, https://www.jpl.nasa.gov/news/news.php?feature=4578.

"Invisible Braces," excerpt from *Health and Medicine*, published on NASA.gov, retrieved February 1, 2018, https://ntrs.nasa.gov/archive/nasa/casi.ntrs.nasa.gov/20020087639.pdf.

Jones, Chris. "Why the International Space Station Is the Single Best Thing We Did," *WIRED*, December 19, 2017, https://www.wired.com/story/why-the-international-space-station-is-the-single-best-thing-we-did.

Moskowitz, Clara. "Horror Stories From Space: 10 Ways Life in Orbit Can Be Rough," Space.com, October 29, 2010, https://www.space.com/9421-horror-stories-space-10-ways-life-in-orbit-rough.html.

NASA. "International Cooperation," NASA.gov, page last updated October 17, 2017, https://www.nasa.gov/mission_pages/station/cooperation/index.html.

NASA. "International Space Station Basics," NASA.gov, retrieved February 14, 2018, https://www.nasa.gov/pdf/179225main_ISS_Poster_Back.pdf.

NASA Technology Transfer Program. "Monitoring Outpatient Care," NASA Spinoff, retrieved February 1, 2018, https://spinoff.nasa.gov/spinoff2003/hm_10.html.

NASA Technology Transfer Program. "Nutritional Products from Space Research," NASA Spinoff, retrieved February 1, 2018, https://spinoff.nasa.gov/spinoff1996/42.html.

National Aeronautics and Space Administration. "About Project Mercury," NASA, last updated August 3, 2017, https://www.nasa.gov/mission_pages/mercury/missions/program-toc.html.

National Aeronautics and Space Administration. "Spinoff 2017," NASA Technology Transfer Program, 2017, https://spinoff.nasa.gov/Spinoff2017/pdf/Spinoff2017.pdf.

National Aeronautics and Space Administration. "Spinoff 2018," NASA Technology Transfer Program, 2018, https://spinoff.nasa.gov/Spinoff2018/pdf/Spinoff2018.pdf.

"Nowruz: Background," United Nations, retrieved January 28, 2018, http://www.un.org/en/events/nowruzday/background.shtml.

Petersen, Carolyn Collins. "Space Exploration Pays Off Here on Earth," ThoughtCo., July 11, 2017, https://www.thoughtco.com/how-does-space-exploration-benefit-you-4082538.

Price, Massoume. "Chahar-Shanbeh Soori," The Circle of Ancient Iranian Studies, retrieved February 5, 2018, http://www.cais-soas.com/CAIS/Celebrations/fire_festival.htm.

"Spring Equinox–Vernal Equinox," Timeanddate.com, retrieved February 5, 2018, https://www.timeanddate.com/calendar/spring-equinox.html.

Werries, Maria. "Space Food," National Aeronautics and Space Administration, July 18, 2016, https://www.nasa.gov/aeroresearch/resources/artifact-opportunities/space-food.

Westcott, W.L. "Resistance training is medicine: effects of strength training on health," *Current Sports Medicine Report*, 11(4), 2012, 209–216, https://www.ncbi.nlm.nih.gov/pubmed/22777332.

VideoOfTheWeekdotCom. "Landing on Titan," YouTube video, 4 min 13 sec, September 1, 2011, https://www.youtube.com/watch?v=0KU9m6MqeXc.

CHAPTER 6: KIMIA ALIZADEH

Alizadeh, Kimia (@kimiya.alizade). 2020. Instagram photo, January 11, 2020, https://www.instagram.com/p/B7LtxeOnZZU/?utm_source=ig_web_copy_link.

BBC. "BBC 100 Women 2019: Who is on the list this year?" *BBC News*, October 16, 2019, https://www.bbc.com/news/world-50042279#:~:text=Kimia%20Alizadeh&text=In%202016%2C%20Kimia%20became%20the,the%20UK%27s%20Financial%20Times%20newspaper.

Bellware, Kim. "The only woman to win an Olympic medal for Iran just defected," *The Seattle Times*, January 12, 2020, https://www.seattletimes.com/nation-world/world/the-only-woman-to-win-an-olympic-medal-for-iran-just-defected/#:~:text=After%20Alizadeh%202016%20Olympic%20victory,told%20reporters%20at%20the%20time.

Bozorgmehr, Najmeh. "Kimia Alizadeh, the Iranian Olympic medallist fighting inequality," *Financial Times*, October 10, 2017, https://www.ft.com/content/cf502dd6-7c26-11e7-ab01-a13271d1ee9c.

Cotovio, Vasco. "Iran's sole female Olympic medalist says she's defected," *CNN*, January 12, 2020, https://www.cnn.com/2020/01/12/middleeast/iran-kimia-alizadeh-defects/index.html.

Ellingworth, James. "After defecting, Iran's only female Olympic medalist seeks new life in Germany," *The Times of Israel*, January 25, 2020, https://www.timesofisrael.com/after-defecting-irans-only-female-olympic-medalist-seeks-new-life-in-germany.

Hohmann, James, host. "An Iranian woman's defection is a reminder of how much people dislike the regime in Tehran," The Daily 202's Big Idea (podcast), January 13, 2020, https://podcasts.apple.com/us/podcast/iranian-womans-defection-is-reminder-how-much-people/id1257234332?i=1000462351310.

"Kimia Alizadeh to undergo knee injury," *Tehran Times*, July 4, 2017, https://www.tehrantimes.com/news/414790/Kimia-Alizadeh-to-undergo-knee-injury.

Rhoades, Tiffany (host). "Kimia Alizadeh," Great Girls (podcast), September 2, 2020, https://podcasts.apple.com/us/podcast/kimia-alizadeh/id1517648575?i=1000489866195.

Ruptly. "Germany: Iran's only female Olympic medalist says she wants to compete for Germany," YouTube, 51 sec, January 24, 2020, https://www.youtube.com/watch?v=Di2We6he5iw.

Specia, Megan. "Iran's Only Female Olympic Medalist Defects Over 'Lies' and 'Injustice,'" *The New York Times*, January 14, 2020, https://www.nytimes.com/2020/01/13/world/middleeast/kimia-alizadeh-iran-defection.html.

World Taekwon Media. "Iranian star Alizadeh could change nationality and compete for Netherlands," posted by epau84, WTM website, January 10, 2020, https://www.wtkmedia.com/taekwondo-iranian-star-alizadeh-could-change-nationality-and-compete-for-netherlands.

World Taekwon Media. "Kimia Alizadeh considering retirement," posted by epau84, WTM website, August 17, 2018, https://www.wtkmedia.com/taekwondo-kimia-alizadeh-considering-retirement.

CHAPTER 7: SHIRIN EBADI

Ayed, Nahlah. "Human rights advocate Shirin Ebadi says the current protests hint at an eventual collapse of Iran's regime," Ideas (podcast), December 26, 2019, https://podcasts.apple.com/us/podcast/human-rights-advocate-shirin-ebadi-says-current-protests/id151485663?i=1000460928488.

Ebadi, Shirin. Interviewed by Amy Goodman. "Iranian Nobel Peace Prize Laureate on Nuclear Deal, Islamic State, Women's Rights," Democracy Now, April 28, 2015, https://www.democracynow.org/2015/4/28/iranian_nobel_peace_prize_laureate_shirin.

Ebadi, Shirin. "Nobel Peace Prize Acceptance Speech," International Federation for Human Rights, January 16, 2004, https://www.fidh.org/en/issues/globalisation-human-rights/economic-social-and-cultural-rights/Speech-by-Shirin-EBADI-Nobel-Peace.

Ebadi, Shirin. *Until We Are Free,* New York: Random House, 2016.

Khakpour, Porochista. "Shirin Ebadi: 'Almost a fourth of the people on Earth are Muslim. Are they like each other? Of course not,'" *The Guardian,* April 25, 2017, https://www.theguardian.com/global-development-professionals-network/2017/apr/25/shirin-ebadi-outside-of-iran-i-knew-id-be-more-useful-i-could-speak.

Mjos, Ole Danbolt, Chairman of the Norwegian Nobel Committee. "Presentation Speech for the 2003 Nobel Peace Prize," Oslo, December 10, 2004, https://www.nobelprize.org/prizes/peace/2003/ceremony-speech.

"Shirin Ebadi," American Program Bureau, Inc., retrieved September 3, 2020, https://www.apbspeakers.com/speaker/shirin-ebadi.

"The Nobel Peace Prize 2003," NobelPrize.org, Nobel Media AB 2020, September 3, 2020, www.nobelprize.org/prizes/peace/2003/summary.

CHAPTER 8: MELODY EHSANI

BahaiTeachings.org. "Your True Calling Might Require a Break from Tradition | Melody Ehsani," YouTube, 17 min 10 sec, March 20, 2017, https://www.youtube.com/watch?v=4Q4EaN3JUfs.

Behind the Hustle. "Cool People With Cool Jobs — Melody Ehsani," YouTube, 4 min 16 sec, January 25, 2012, https://www.youtube.com/watch?v=HEzYg6b2fDY.

Dan Deutsch Optical Outlook. "Jewelry Designer Melody Ehsani on Craftmanship," YouTube, 3 min 11 sec, May 23, 2013, https://www.youtube.com/watch?v=lffxXe0n4W8.

McGloster, Niki. "I Want Your Job: Melody Ehsani, Jewelry and Fashion Designer," Elite Daily, December 10, 2015, https://www.elitedaily.com/women/want-your-job-melody-ehsani-fashion/1313374#:~:text=I%20was%20raised%20in%20the,way%20to%20express%20her%20passion.

MissCrewTV. "MISS Interviews Melody Ehsani," YouTube, 4 min 20 sec, March 26, 2013, https://www.youtube.com/watch?v=K-LqLg66FEU.

Moinzadeh, Attoosa. "Why It's Important Now, More Than Ever, To Celebrate Norooz," *Fader,* March 20, 2017, https://www.thefader.com/2017/03/20/norooz-melody-ehsani-iranian-bahai-interview#:~:text=Attributing%20much%20of%20this%20to,their%20homes%20away%20from%20home.

Nike. "Behind the Design: Melody Ehsani," Nike.com, retrieved September 3, 2020, https://www.nike.com/launch/t/behind-the-design-melody-ehsani.

Nike. "The Women's Dunk, Disrupted," Nike Sportswear press release, August 21, 2020, https://news.nike.com/footwear/nike-dunk-low-disrupt-official-images-release-date.

Schlemmer, Zack. "Melody Ehsani and Hassan Hajjaj Design the Reebok Court Victory Pump," Sneaker News, February 9, 2017, https://sneakernews.com/2017/02/09/melody-ehsani-hassan-hajjaj-reebok-court-victory-pump-valentines-day.

Schlemmer, Zack. "Melody Ehsani x Reebok Question Mid," Sneaker News, November 29, 2016, https://sneakernews.com/2016/11/29/melody-ehsani-reebok-question-mid.

Sneaker Stories, "Nike Air Jordan 1–Mid–Melody Ehsani–Fearless (Review + On Foot)," YouTube, 7 min 52 sec, December 17, 2019, https://www.youtube.com/watch?v=Me0MInvdZxY.

Sole DXB. "Melody Ehsani—Discovering my divine blueprint in art + design at Sole DXB 2017," YouTube, 51 min 55 sec, February 27, 2018, https://www.youtube.com/watch?v=Si24eRXNxGs.

Staple, Jeff, host. "Episode 6: Melody Ehsani," Business of Hype (podcast), March 25, 2018, retrieved September 3, 2020, https://podcasts.apple.com/us/podcast/melody-ehsani/id1242776507?i=1000407436242.

CHAPTER 9: FARNAZ ESMAEILZADEH

Esmaeilzadeh, Farnaz. Interviewed by Yasmine Mahdavi on July 29, 2020.

Esmaeilzadeh, Farnaz. Email exchange with Yasmine Mahdavi on August 10, 2020.

Lubben, Alex. "A Portrait in Speed: Iranian Speed Climber Farnaz Esmaeilzadeh," Climbing, October 27, 2017, updated May 31, 2018, https://www.climbing.com/people/a-portrait-in-speed-iranian-speed-climber-farnaz-esmaeilzadeh.

Press TV Doc. "Farnaz Esmaeilzadeh," Press TV, 50 min 29 sec, retrieved September 3, 2020, http://presstvdoc.com/post/14682.

TEDx Talks. "The True Power of Courage | Farnaz Esmaeilzadeh | TEDxSari," YouTube, 12 min 37 sec, October 3, 2017, https://www.youtube.com/watch?v=fiTl9jVs_3k&feature=youtu.be.

CHAPTER 10: GOLSHIFTEH FARAHANI

Das, Ria. "Golshifteh Farahani: Who Is This Iranian Born Extraction Actor?" SheThePeople, April 28, 2020, https://www.shethepeople.tv/top-stories/golshifteh-farahani-extraction-iranian-born-actor.

Farahani, Golshifteh. Interviewed by Christopher Gates. "Actress Golshifteh Farahani dishes on Netflix's Extraction," Looper, May 5, 2020, https://www.looper.com/207120/actress-golshifteh-farahani-dishes-on-netflixs-extraction-exclusive-interview.

Farahani, Golshifteh. Interviewed by Namrata Joshi. "All my inspiration is from my longing for Iran," The Hindu, January 9, 2016, https://www.thehindu.com/opinion/op-ed/%E2%80%98All-my-inspiration-is-from-my-longing-for-Iran%E2%80%99/article13990267.ece.

France 24 English. "Golshifteh Farahani: An Iranian Actress in Exile," YouTube, 11 min 26 sec, February 11, 2020, https://www.youtube.com/watch?v=gcVP2sIQV-w.

"Kooch Neshin: Biography," Last.FM, retrieved September 23, 2020, https://www.last.fm/music/Kooch+Neshin/+wiki.

Moore, Camille. "10 Things You Didn't Know About Golshifteh Farahani," TVOvermind, retrieved September 23, 2020, https://www.tvovermind.com/golshifteh-farahani.

Official Ahang Farsi. "Golshifteh Farahani—Joz to OFFICIAL SOUND," YouTube, 4 min 40 sec, December 24, 2015, https://www.youtube.com/watch?v=y9s-JZYyTSc.

OnePress TV. "Golshifteh Farahani: 'They didn't want to be killed by a woman,'" YouTube, 2 min 26 sec, May 14, 2018, https://www.youtube.com/watch?v=awQOJA2gong.

Phillips, Patrick. "Why Nik from *Extraction* looks so familiar," Looper, April 17, 2020, https://www.looper.com/202521/why-nik-from-extraction-looks-so-familiar.

Sanil, Sharan. "All We Know About the Talented Golshifteh Farahani From *Extraction* Who Stole Our Hearts," MensXP, April 27, 2020, https://www.mensxp.com/social-hits/news/75584-facts-about-golshifteh-farahani-actress-from-netflix-movie-extraction.html.

The Hollywood Reporter. "Live From Cannes: My Sweet Pepperland," YouTube, 3 min 9 sec, May 28, 2013, https://www.youtube.com/watch?v=uVvawRfjw6Y.

Vaziri, Ryan. "Creative License: *Paterson*'s Golshifteh Farahani Talks Jarmusch and Breaking Through Iranian Self-Censorship," MovieMaker, December 26, 2016, https://www.moviemaker.com/jim-jarmusch-paterson-golshifteh-farahani.

CHAPTER 11: NIAZ KASRAVI

ACLU. "Racial Profiling: Definition," ACLU.org, retrieved September 23, 2020, https://www.aclu.org/other/racial-profiling-definition.

"Avalan Institute," Avalan Institute, retrieved September 3, 2020, https://www.avalaninstitute.com.

Center for Iranian Diaspora Studies. "Dr. Niaz Kasravi, Justice Advocate, Founder Avalan Institute," YouTube, 2 min 54 sec, March 21, 2019, https://www.youtube.com/watch?v=YCTTHahtulM.

Kasravi, Niaz. Email exchange with Yasmine Mahdavi on August 12, 2020.

Kasravi, Niaz. Interviewed by Yasmine Mahdavi on July 30, 2020.

NAACP Randolph County. 2012. "Six years ago, John McNeil received a call from his son that changed John's life," Facebook, September 28, 2012, https://www.facebook.com/117164218410594/posts/six-years-ago-john-mcneil-received-a-call-from-his-son-that-changed-johns-life-e/235220293271652.

Zeine, Dr. Foojan. "Bright & Elevated Way—Dr. Foojan Zeine interviews Dr. Niaz Kasravi & Diana Rowan," YouTube, 55 min 47 sec, June 10, 2020, https://www.youtube.com/watch?v=2lVc3uERbjM.

CHAPTER 12: KATAYOUN KHOSROWYAR

Burgoyne, Bethany. "Katayoun Khosrowyar: The Iranian Coach on a Mission," Reform the Funk, retrieved September 3, 2020, https://www.

reformthefunk.com/features/katayoun-khosrowyar-the-iranian-coach-on-a-mission.

FIFA, "The coach transforming IR Iran's Women's Game," FIFA.com, October 30, 2018, https://www.fifa.com/womens-football/news/the-coach-transforming-ir-iran-s-women-s-game.

"FIFA president calls for skimpy uniforms," China Daily, January 17, 2004, http://www.chinadaily.com.cn/en/doc/2004-01/17/content_299751.htm.

Jackson, Melanie, et al. "Was the FIFA president wrong to suggest women soccer players wear tighter shorts?" ESPN Writers' Bloc, retrieved September 3, 2020, http://www.espn.com/page2/s/bloc/040120.html.

Khosrowyar, Katayoun. Email exchange with Yasmine Mahdavi on August 17, 2020.

Khosrowyar, Katayoun. Interviewed by Lulu Garcia-Navarro. "Protests Against Ban on Women at Men's Soccer Games in Iran," NPR, September 15, 2019, https://www.npr.org/2019/09/15/760936519/protests-against-ban-on-women-at-mens-soccer-games-in-iran.

Khosrowyar, Katayoun. Interviewed by Marjan Golpira. "Nothing can hold down Iran's female footballers: Katayoun Khosrowyar," Tehran Times, December 25, 2018, https://www.tehrantimes.com/news/431080/Nothing-can-hold-down-Iran-s-female-footballers-Katayoun-Khosrowyar.

Khosrowyar, Katayoun. Interviewed by Yasmine Mahdavi on August 10, 2020.

Mortazavi, Negar. "Katayoun Khosrowyar: Meet the Iranian-American athlete leading a football revolution," Independent Premium, June 3, 2019, https://www.independent.co.uk/independentminds/long-reads/katayoun-khosrowyar-iran-america-womens-football-profile-a8886496.html.

"NYC Majlis with Katayoun 'Kat' Khosrowyar," Eventbrite.com, retrieved September 3, 2020, https://www.eventbrite.com/e/nyc-majlis-with-katayoun-kat-khosrowyar-tickets-115818617603?aff=erelexpmlt#.

Stahl, Lesley. "2016: Lesley Stahl reports on women's soccer in Iran," CBS video, 14 min 58 sec, October 9, 2019, https://www.cbs.com/shows/60_minutes/video/4AA_gqlc5mcQEXBkmQxiL_eH3zOExRyp/2016-lesley-stahl-reports-on-women-s-soccer-in-iran.

CHAPTER 13: MARYAM MIRZAKHANI

BBC Persian. "Algebra Girl: The Life of Maryam Mirzakhani, Iranian Mathematician," YouTube, 27 min 33 sec, September 5, 2018, https://www.youtube.com/watch?v=IP3ZiBBntHE.

Collins, Tara, et al (hosts). "Maryam Mirzakhani," Girls Talk Math (podcast), https://podcasts.apple.com/us/podcast/maryam-mirzakhani/id1171540798?i=1000389920169.

Csicsery, George. Secrets of the Surface: The Mathematical Vision of Maryam Mirzakhani. Directed by George Csicsery. (2020; Zala Films), film, http://www.zalafilms.com/secrets.

Harford, Tim (host). "Maryam Mirzakhani — A Genius of Maths," More or Less: Behind the Statistics (podcast), BBC 4 Radio, July 24, 2017, https://podcasts.apple.com/us/podcast/maryam-mirzakhani-a-genius-of-maths/id267300884?i=1000390243930.

Lamb, Evelyn. "Mathematics World Mourns Maryam Mirzakhani, Only Woman to Win Fields Medal," Scientific American, July 17, 2017, https://

www.scientificamerican.com/article/mathematics-world-mourns-maryam-mirzakhani-only-woman-to-win-fields-medal.

Lockhart, Paul. *A Mathematician's Lament: How School Cheats Us Out of Our Most Fascinating and Imaginative Art Form.* New York: Bellevue Literary Press, 2009.

Math Union. "The Work of Maryam Mirzakhani," MathUnion.org news release, retrieved September 30, 2020, https://www.mathunion.org/fileadmin/IMU/Prizes/Fields/2014/news_release_mirzakhani.pdf.

Obituary of Maryam Mirzakhani. "Maryam Mirzakhani died on July 14," *The Economist*, July 20, 2017, https://www.economist.com/obituary/2017/07/20/obituary-maryam-mirzakhani-died-on-july-14th?zid=311&ah=308cac674cccf554ce65cf926868bbc2.

Shahriari, Shahriar. William Polk Russell Professor of Mathematics at Pomona College. Email exchange with Yasmine Mahdavi on July 29, 2020.

CHAPTER 14: SHIRIN NESHAT

Abel-Hirsch, Hannah. "Shirin Neshat: Unraveling the American Dream," British Journal of Photography, June 18, 2020, https://www.bjp-online.com/2020/06/shirin-neshat-unraveling-the-american-dream.

Alemdar, Melis. "Looking for Oum Kulthum: Shirin Neshat brings a legend to the silver screen," TRT World, April 18, 2018, https://www.trtworld.com/magazine/looking-for-oum-kulthum-shirin-neshat-brings-a-legend-to-the-silver-screen-16821.

Balaghi, Shiva. "Reflecting on Shirin Neshat's Career With the Artist's Words," Hyperallergic, January 13, 2020, https://hyperallergic.com/536761/shirin-neshat-broad-museum-i-will-greet-the-sun-again.

Banks, Grace (host). "Grace Banks Interviews Shirin Neshat," Sleek (podcast), April 14, 2020, https://podcasts.apple.com/us/podcast/sleek-podcast-03-grace-banks-interviews-shirin-neshat/id1472791287?i=1000471445117.

Bekhrad, Joobin. "Call to Arms," *Reorient*, February 18, 2013, http://www.reorientmag.com/2013/02/call-to-arms.

Genesis, Chrystal (host). "Politician Bobi Wine; Visual Artist Shirin Neshat; Singer Ghostpoet; Filmmaker Elizabeth Carroll on Diana Kennedy," Stance (podcast), May 1, 2020, https://podcasts.apple.com/us/podcast/politician-bobi-wine-visual-artist-shirin-neshat-singer/id1193648912?i=1000473227391.

Green, Tyler (host). "Shirin Neshat, James Tissot," The Modern Art Notes Podcast (podcast), November 14, 2019, https://podcasts.apple.com/us/podcast/shirin-neshat-james-tissot/id479811154?i=1000456838113.

Hessel, Katy (host). "Shirin Neshat," The Great Women Artists (podcast), February 25, 2020, https://podcasts.apple.com/us/podcast/shirin-neshat/id1480259187?i=1000466570266.

Krysiak, Eva (producer). "Shirin Neshat on the video art that reconnected her with Iran," The Start (podcast), March 22, 2018, https://podcasts.apple.com/us/podcast/shirin-neshat-on-video-art-that-reconnected-her-iran/id1337773497?i=1000407124341.

Miranda, Carolina A. "Artist Shirin Neshat challenges the idea of Muslim women as victims and explores exile," *Los Angeles Times*, October 23, 2019, https://www.latimes.com/entertainment-arts/story/2019-10-23/artist-shirin-neshat-muslim-women-as-victims-exile-iran.

Neshat, Shirin. "Artist Statement," *Signs*, retrieved September 23, 2020, http://signsjournal.org/shirin-neshat.

Radojcin, Danielle (host). "Shirin Neshat," The Collector's House (podcast), February 26, 2020, https://podcasts.apple.com/us/podcast/shirin-neshat/id1431920149?i=1000466732292.

Reeves, Minou. "*Female Warriors of Allah*: Women and the Islamic Revolution," Kirkus Reviews, January 16, 1988, https://www.kirkusreviews.com/book-reviews/a/minou-reeves/female-warriors-of-allah-women-and-the-islamic-/.

"Shirin Neshat," The Guggenheim Museum, retrieved September 23, 2020, https://www.guggenheim.org/artwork/artist/shirin-neshat.

Yerebakan, Osman Can. "Artist Shirin Neshat's advice on simple skin care," *Wallpaper**, May 14, 2020, https://www.wallpaper.com/beauty-grooming/artist-shirin-neshat-simple-skin-care-advise.

Young, Allison. "Shirin Neshat, Rebellious Silence, Women of Allah Series," Khan Academy, retrieved September 23, 2020, https://www.khanacademy.org/humanities/ap-art-history/global-contemporary-apah/20th-century-apah/a/neshat-rebellious#:~:text=Shirin%20Neshat%27s%20photographic%20series%20%22Women,of%20personal%20and%20religious%20conviction.

CHAPTER 15: MARJANE SATRAPI

"About the Author: Marjane Satrapi," Penguin Random House, retrieved September 3, 2020, https://www.penguinrandomhouse.com/authors/43801/marjane-satrapi.

Amanpour & Co. "'Persepolis' Creator Marjane Satrapi Discusses Her New Film," PBS.org video, 1 min 52 sec, July 22, 2020, https://www.pbs.org/wnet/amanpour-and-company/video/persepolis-creator-marjane-satrapi-discusses-her-new-film.

IFC News. "Marjane Satrapi: 'Persepolis' a pro-Iranian humanist tale," YouTube, 3 min 16 sec, October 11, 2007, https://www.youtube.com/watch?v=aMwfzqEqVLk.

Movieweb. "Persepolis–Exclusive: Marjane Satrapi," YouTube, 4 min 2 sec, September 19, 2010, https://www.youtube.com/watch?v=v9onZpQix_w.

New York Public Library. "'How Dostoevsky Changed My Life' | Marjane Satrapi LIVE from the NYPL," YouTube, 2 min 15 sec, November 6, 2014, https://www.youtube.com/watch?v=0FowsmRP6Ak.

Pen America. "Conversation with Marjane Satrapi and Art Speigelman," YouTube, 1 hour 40 min 21 sec, March 13, 2017, https://www.youtube.com/watch?v=rUmSAq5uNLY.

Pen America. "Conversation with Marjane Satrapi," YouTube, 27 min, May 10, 2012, https://www.youtube.com/watch?v=crhUl5zZzi8.

Quirke, Antonia, host. "Marjane Satrapi," The Film Programme (podcast), June 11, 2020, https://podcasts.apple.com/us/podcast/marjane-satrapi/id266569843?i=1000477574974.

Satrapi, Marjane. Interviewed by John Zuarino. "An Interview With Marjane Satrapi,"

Bookslut, November 2006, http://www.bookslut.com/features/2006_11_010204.php.

Satrapi, Marjane. Interviewed by Paul Holdengräber. "Live from the NYPL: Marjane Satrapi," New York Public Library, October 17, 2014, https://www.nypl.org/audiovideo/marjane-satrapi-paul-holdengr%C3%A4ber.

Satrapi, Marjane. *Radioactive.* Directed by Marjane Satrapi. (2020; Amazon Studios), film.

FOOD FOR THOUGHT:
Discussion Guide & Writing Prompts

Chapter 1: Anousheh Ansari

Discussion Guide

- In this chapter, you learned about "brain drain." Discuss how it can impact affected countries—both in countries that lose their citizens and those who receive them.
- Do you have any business ideas? If so, what are the first three steps you would take to execute your idea?
- Despite Anousheh's uncertainties, she took chances. When was the last time you took a chance on something? How did it turn out? Would you do it again? Why?
- In the context of entrepreneurship, think about the differences between being a consumer versus being a producer. Which do you want to be? Why?

Writing Prompt

- How does unrest and insecurity displace civilians? Pick at least one contemporary example from a different region of the world to demonstrate your perspective.
- Write a journal entry in which you imagine living on another planet. How did you get there? What are your daily responsibilities? Do you plan to stay for a long time?
- How did the 1979 Revolution in Iran compare to other revolutions you have studied?
- How do revolutions change society?

Chapter 2: Mina Bissell

Discussion Guide

- How has the study of science led to breakthroughs in medicine? Provide one or two examples.
- Name three other scientists from various social or ethnic backgrounds who have made significant contributions to science. How many are first- or second-generation Americans?
- Determine the core message of the "STEM Pep Talk." Did you find anything surprising? What are your thoughts on the advice provided?
- Pick a time and place in the Middle East. Compare and contrast the experiences of those in the Middle East with the experience that Americans in the U.S. were having at the same time.

Writing Prompt

- Mina struggled with advisers who belittled her and her ideas. Has someone ever underestimated or undervalued you? What did you do? How did you feel? Were you able to change their mind?
- How is your family similar to or different from Mina's?
- Imagine yourself as a scientist. What question would you want to answer?
- Imagine you are a state leader. Make the case to other world leaders about the value of female education in families, communities, and economies.

Chapter 3: Dorsa Derakhshani

Discussion Guide

- List two or three countries that were sanctioned by the U.S. When have sanctions been effective? When have they been ineffective?
- Is assigning "women's titles" in chess or other arenas a good idea? Justify your response.
- How did learning about a woman from the Middle East who mastered the complicated game of chess change your opinion about women from the Middle East?

Writing Prompt
- Pick an authoritarian regime that you have already studied. What impact did that kind of government have on its citizens? Consider the economy, the press, and the judiciary as examples to study more deeply.
- Imagine you are the president of your country. Write a speech answering the following question: When, if ever, is it morally justified to discern between people when determining whom to allow in your country?

Chapter 4: Anna Eskamani

Discussion Guide
- How can you be a good citizen without being politically or civically involved?
- Why do you have to differentiate between fact and fiction when it comes to news and information sources? How do you do this?
- Do you think it is important to advocate for your rights and the rights of those different from you — those who don't look like you, act like you, or come from the same place as you? Why?
- President John F. Kennedy famously said, "The rights of every man are diminished when the rights of one man are threatened." How would you respond to this quote?
- Dr. Martin Luther King, Jr. once said, "…I submit that an individual who breaks a law that conscience tells him is unjust, and who willingly accepts the penalty of imprisonment in order to arouse the conscience of the community over its injustice, is in reality expressing the highest respect for law." What do you think about this quote?

Writing Prompt
- Who is responsible for ensuring that your rights are preserved? Why do you think this individual(s) or institution(s) holds this power?
- Many times, Anna felt like an outsider. Has anyone made you feel unwelcomed? Do you know why they wanted to make you feel that way? How did you overcome that feeling?
- When Anna was in the fifth grade, she wrote a petition to keep her lunch period with her best friend. If you could wish for

something to be different in your school or community, what would it be? How would you go about getting your voice heard?

- In your class, have each student write a newspaper article about one recent event. Compare and contrast how each of you interpreted the event and how you chose to convey the message to your audience. How did the information vary among your classmates? Did you find any bias?

- What is voter suppression? Find an example of a community or group that has either suffered or gained from voter suppression and explain how and why they were suppressed or otherwise, as well the effect it had on the lives of the members.

Chapter 5: Jasmin Moghbeli

Discussion Guide

- Jasmin competed against a strong pool of applicants when she applied to become a NASA astronaut. Have you ever competed? How did you feel about it?

- Jasmin joined the Marines as a stepping stone to achieve another goal, to become an astronaut. How have you been creative in finding ways to achieve your goals? Did your strategy work? If not, what would you do differently now?

- Jasmin's parents converted from Islam to Christianity. In the news, we learn that more Muslim refugees are converting to Christianity. Find an example in history when a persecuted people converted to other religions. Why do you think this happened? How did it benefit or hurt those who converted?

- How have immigrants made contributions to American society? Provide examples of three individuals, detailing where they came from, what they contributed, and how they influenced our society.

Writing Prompt

- Jasmin used to be afraid of public speaking, but with repeated practice she overcame her fear. Give an example of how you once overcame a fear.

- How do innovations in military technology provide improvements to the life of civilians?

- In January 2017, President Trump signed an executive order called "Protecting the Nation from Foreign Terrorist Entry in

the United States," commonly referred to as "the Muslim Ban." This ban barred citizens of seven majority-Muslim countries from visiting the U.S. With your teacher, read the executive order and its subsequent forms. What do you know now that you didn't before? Write two essays, one as an opponent to and the other as a proponent for this ban. Refer to the Anti-Defamation League's Current Events Classroom, "The Muslim Ban and the Power of Protest," for more information. https://www.adl.org/media/9731/download
- Do you think military service should be compulsory? Justify your response.

Chapter 6: Kimia Alizadeh
- In history, there have been many athletes who defected from their country of birth. Find out who they are and why they left.

Chapter 7: Shirin Ebadi
- Who would you nominate for the next Nobel Peace Prize, and why?

Chapter 8: Melody Ehsani
- There is more than one way to achieve a goal. What variations have you tried to overcome a challenge?

Chapter 9: Farnaz Esmaeilzadeh
- Do you want to start something that no one around you has ever done before? What would it be, and how would you get there?

Chapter 10: Golshifteh Farahani
- Learn about an artist living in exile whose work you admire.

Chapter 11: Niaz Kasravi
- Why is it important to protect the right to dissent?

Chapter 12: Katayoun Khosrowyar
- Research those who cannot take part in an activity that's readily available to you. Why are there barriers to their participation?

Chapter 13: Maryam Mirzakhani
- Draw a link between art, in any medium, and your latest challenging math assignment.

Chapter 14: Shirin Neshat
- Create a work of art, in any medium, that interprets your explanation of a paradox.

Chapter 15: Marjane Satrapi
- Write a seven-word autobiography in the form of haiku: the first line has five syllables, the second has seven, and the third has five.

A NOTE ON THE ART

The illustrations in this book were created by the following talented women with roots in the Middle East.

Stephanie Badr illustrated Kimia Alizadeh, Mina Bissell, Melody Ehsani, and Katayoun Khosrowyar. Stephanie was born in Lebanon. Stephanie loves to challenge herself. She hopes that every girl finds the courage to strive. Instagram: @stephaniebadr

Samar Chahine illustrated Anousheh Ansari and Dorsa Derakhshani. Samar was born in California and raised in Southern Lebanon. She began taking commissions in 2017 for graphite realistic portraits and currently works with multiple media. Instagram: @chahine_illustration

Rosane Chawi illustrated Shirin Ebadi, Farnaz Esmaeilzadeh, and Maryam Mirzakhani. Rosane is a Lebanese illustrator who loves working with bright colors and creating visuals that take her to another world. Instagram: @rosanechawi

Sahar Haghgoo illustrated Golshifteh Farahani, Shirin Neshat, and Marjane Satrapi. Sahar was born in Iran. She holds an MA in Illustration from the University of Tehran. Sahar works as an illustrator and painter in England. Instagram: @sahar__haghgoo

Christelle Halal illustrated Jasmin Moghbeli, Niaz Kasravi, and "ACT (ivism)". Christelle was born in Lebanon and received an MA in Illustration from the Lebanese Academy of Fine Arts, where she also teaches. She has illustrated several children's books. Instagram: @christellehalal

Zaynab Kadri illustrated Anna Eskamani and Yasmine Mahdavi. Zaynab is a Lebanese artist who was born and raised in the U.S. She graduated with a degree in graphic design. Surrealism, vintage arts, and cartoons are her favorites. Instagram: @zaynabgrimink

Dalida Raad illustrated "Iran-Iraq War," "Pep-Talk," "Women in Chess," "Veiled," "Notable Women," "Life on the ISS," "Nowruz," and "Space Studies." Dalida is based in Lebanon and Oman. She graduated with a degree in graphic design from the American University of Beirut. Dalida uses her creative skills to raise awareness about meaningful issues. Instagram: @dalistrations

A NOTE ON THE RESEARCH

Work on this project began in the fall of 2017. I interviewed some of the women in this book. I read books, interviews, and articles written by them or about them. I watched many films, documentaries, and interviews they have made or given. I followed and reviewed their social media postings. I read primary, secondary, and tertiary sources. I also consulted technical experts and scholars for further accuracy. Some of the women read what I wrote about them. In all instances, I made every effort to present factual, well-researched stories of real women without being controversial or scandalous. My sources for the chapters and respective sidebars are cited.

ACKNOWLEDGMENTS

My deepest gratitude to all who traveled this writing journey with me. This book has been made possible with the care, generosity, guidance, kindness, critique, mentorship, and love of many.

Thank you to all of my family and friends who dared to imagine this dream with me. My husband and children, for their infinite patience, continuous encouragement, and editing and critique. My parents, who pushed me to finish writing this book even when I was losing hope. My big, Iranian family — sister, brother-in-law, uncles, aunts, and first, second, third, and fourth cousins — who cheered me along and believed in me. My friends whose encouragement and curiosity inspired me. To those of you who read early chapter drafts, I am grateful. The questions, ideas, wisdom, knowledge, and confidence from all of you made this project possible. My special tween and teen early-beta readers, Makeda Faxio and Juliette Carasso, for their special insight. My late uncle's endless curiosity about this book stays close to my heart.

To trailblazers Anousheh Ansari, Mina Bissell, Dorsa Derakhshani, Anna Eskamani, Farnaz Esmaeilzadeh, Katayoun Khosrowyar, Niaz Kasravi, and Shirin Neshat for giving me their time.

To the illustrators Stephanie Badr, Samar Chahine, Rosane Chawi, Sahar Haghgoo, Christelle Halal, Zaynab Kadri, and Dalida Raad. Your illustrations make the book dazzle.

To Jaime deBlanc-Knowles for all of your editorial magic, from the start.

To all of the judges at We Need Diverse Books for granting me the 2018 Walter Grant Award. You propelled my vision forward.

To Quressa Robinson for your invaluable and thoughtful guidance.

To the Society of Children's Book Writers and Illustrators (SCBWI) for awarding me the Nevada Mentorship in 2019. Jenny MacKay for your extraordinary mentorship and direction. Sharon Eberhardt and Josey Goggin for your encouragement and wise feedback.

This book was published amid a global pandemic that has touched every corner of our lives. Its sobering impact has again unearthed the ways our brethren are shackled and choked worldwide. I find solace in the tenacity of those who persevere nonetheless. I hope that we all seize this time to reflect and find ways to be a positive influence in each other's lives.

Finally, to my readers, thank you, thank you for inviting this book into your life. Your curiosity and, most importantly, your imagination are priceless.

ABOUT THE AUTHOR

Yasmine Mahdavi was born and raised in Iran. She left Iran for the U.S. when she was twelve years old. Her career has spanned both the nonprofit and corporate sectors. She wrote this book — her first — to her thirteen-year-old self as an homage to her country of birth and an ode to her adopted country. Yasmine is the recipient of a 2018 We Need Diverse Books Walter Grant Award and a 2019 Society of Children's Book Writers and Illustrators (SCBWI) Nevada Mentorship. Yasmine lives in New York City with her husband, their two children, and a rescue Labrador Retriever.